CATS
The Love They Give Us

CATS
The Love They Give Us

Susan DeVore Williams

Fleming H. Revell Company
Tarrytown, New York

Unless otherwise indicated, Scripture quotations in this book are taken from the King James Version of the Bible.

Scripture quotations identified AMP are from AMPLIFIED BIBLE, OLD TESTAMENT, Copyright 1962, 1964 by Zondervan Publishing House and are used by permission.

Library of Congress Cataloging-in-Publication Data

Cats: the love they give us / [edited by] Susan DeVore Williams.
    p. cm.
  ISBN 0-8007-1593-4 : $9.95
    1. Cats. 2. Cats—Anecdotes. 3. Cats—Literary collections.
4. Cats—Religious aspects—Christianity.   I. Williams, Susan
DeVore.
SF445.5.C4   1988
818'.02—dc19   88-4541
                                                                   CIP

Printed in the United States of America

This book is for my dad,
Dr. Hugh ("Pidge") Williams of Sparta, Wisconsin,
who taught me to care about animals—
and made me love to tell stories as much as he does.

I'm especially indebted to friends—both old and new—whose enthusiasm about this project made my work a little easier. To name them all would be impossible. A few deserve medals: Lee Lofaro of *Guideposts*; Martha Moore; Dr. Michael Fox; Marjorie Holmes; Rebecca and Randy True; Christian veterinary students of the Unviersity of California at Davis; Bill Kennedy of Friends of Animals in New York; Dale Walden of the Pet Food Institute in Washington, D.C.; Revell staff and friends and my own family and friends who graciously provided snapshots of their pets; Karen Staps-Walters and the teachers and students of Sacramento Country Day School; Mrs. Jones and her students at Florin Christian Academy of Sacramento; Mrs. Orr and her teachers at Capital Christian School in Sacramento. And an extra big hug for my husband, Richard Kirkham.

"I can't fix dinner yet, Fluffy is still asleep."

Contents

*T*he behavior of men to animals and their behavior to each other bear a constant relationship.
　　　　　　　　　　　　　　　　　　—Herbert Spencer

Introduction

I'm an easy woman to get along with—normally. I'm kind, forgiving, and warmhearted—or at least that's what my husband tells me, and he wouldn't lie. I'm cranky only on the rarest occasions. And I never argue. Well, almost never.

But there's this single, well-defined area in my life that I've come to regard as something of a mine field. I mean, if you put your foot on the wrong spot in there, you're likely to hear a gigantic explosion—just before you're hit by the shrapnel.

That area is where the animals hang out. Not just *my* animals, you understand—*all* animals. For as long as I can remember, I've acted like the Joan of Arc—I mean *Ark*—of the animal world. I've been known to leap from moving cars to rescue injured dogs and cats, to climb tall trees to replace a fallen chick from a sparrow's nest, and to threaten to break the knees of terrified little boys I've caught in the act of stoning frogs in a pond. Once I even challenged a dognapper who threatened me with a gun as he held a choking dog on a rope in his other hand—and I won! I won't get into it, but I'll admit it gave me trembling spasms in my elbows for a week. It's not easy to be Joan of Ark.

My problems over animals may be genetic. My eighty-three-year-old father, "Pidge" Williams, is an old-fashioned country doctor with a rare gift for storytelling and a profound love and compassion for animals. As a result, many of the stories I remember from my Wisconsin childhood were true-life animal stories that could only come from small-town and rural America.

A few of Dad's old patients still remember the day Dave Jenkins's dog was hit by a car. Dave called Dad right away, asking if he could bring the dog to the clinic to be X-rayed. Dad suggested he take the dog to the town vet, but Dave would have none of that. "I don't want a *vet*," he said. "This is my *dog*, for Pete's sake! I want our family doctor!"

How could Dad refuse such a plea? He agreed to look at the dog, and within a few minutes Dave arrived with the dog. Dad and his nurse met them, and the three of them carried the pitiful pooch through the crowded waiting area into an exam room. There an X ray showed that there were no broken bones. The dog lived for some years after that.

That was in the 1940s or '50s the best I can remember, but people still see my dad on the street from time to time and say, "Doc, I remember the day Dave Jenkins carried his dog through your waiting room," and they'll trade stories for a while.

There was also the story about Marv Libke and his plothound. (I never knew what a plothound was, exactly, but there seemed to be a lot of them around our area.) As my dad explained it, Marv loved this dog like a baby. It went everywhere with him, and when Dad went to Marv's house, the dog was always treated like one of the family.

One afternoon while Dad was at the clinic he got a frantic call from Marv. The dog had jumped a fence, he said, and a foot-long reed had run up his leg. Marv had taken him to the vet, but after much probing the vet simply couldn't get it out. Reeds have a structure a lot like a giant foxtail, and when they go in, they grip the flesh like a toggle bolt. Marv begged my dad to come right over to his house and give it one more try.

Naturally, he did. The dog was in a lot of pain, but Dad quickly saw that the reed was not going to come out the way it had gone in. He made an incision twelve inches above the entry point and managed to pull it out in one piece—all without much pain to the dog. As he held up the bloody reed, he saw that Marv's face was covered with tears. "I never saw him cry before or after that day," Dad says. The dog recovered without incident, and my dad has always claimed it was one of his most satisfying pieces of surgery.

I heard for years about Dad's childhood animal experiences. His mother died just after he was born, and a few years later, when his father remarried, he was sent off to live with relatives and friends because his stepmother simply didn't want him around. Dad spent summers on the farms of various relatives and winters with others who agreed to take him in for a time. He adapted well to his itinerant life-style—partly, I'd guess, because most of the places he lived had animals that were a predictable source of affection. One home had a cat that Dad named Tige— short for Tiger. The cat always slept under the covers at the foot of his bed, keeping him warm on cold nights. At another house, a pet squirrel lived in his pocket most of one summer. With all the assorted tame and wild animals he got to know, Dad's often said it's a wonder he didn't die of rabies or mange.

Anyway, I guess I come by my passion for animals honestly. I might as well go ahead and be passionate—after all, if it's genetic, there's nothing I can do about it anyway.

For years of my adult life I worked to help animals on a one-at-a-time basis. Strays seemed to pass the word among themselves that I was an easy mark, and they hunted me down with remarkable persistence. When I lived in Minneapolis, a dog I'd never seen found its way into my office at the University of Minnesota Health Sciences Center, and through several closed corridors to my desk, where he immediately put down roots. It was during those years that I became the first person in history to be treated by the University Health Service for a squirrel bite— which was the result of my attempts to hand-feed Planter's Cocktail Peanuts to the little guy who begged at my office window.

In Folsom, California, where I lived for a couple of years on an isolated bluff on the American River, my name must have been scribbled on fire hydrants. Stray dogs found me everywhere—at the grocery store, on the way to church, and even in the parking lot of a laundromat, where a skinny, filthy dog I named Buddy dramatically threw himself in front of my parked car and collapsed.

It was also in Folsom that I got involved with Gordon Brong and his now-famous "Misfit Zoo"—a collection of injured and orphaned animals that could not be returned to the wild and were brought to Gordon one at a time because he was known as a compassionate animal lover. I volunteered for a year or two to help Gordon muck out cages and feed the zoo's population. In exchange, Gordon taught me about the real world of the animals, as opposed to the world I'd read about and experienced in my sheltered existence in cities. It was an experience I'll always treasure—in spite of the fact that I've never quite recovered from being singled out (in a way I'm not allowed to describe in print) as the love object of the zoo's Siberian tiger. As I say, it's not easy to be Joan of Ark.

Through all of this, of course, my own pets have loved me, taught me, encouraged me, and bled me dry, which is what pets are supposed to do, I guess. They've wrung out my emotions and carried me to the heights and depths the human spirit is capable of surviving—all without a hint of apology. Not that I expected one. Animals tend to become arrogant about their status when they live with me.

Of course, after years of this kind of thing, there was only one thing left for me to do. I had to write a pet book. I've been threatening to do it for years. Only last night I got caught up in an argument with one of my best, most belligerent Christian friends—a gun-toting lawman who likes to say that "God looks at animals the way He looks at rocks and trees—as decorative, but of no value except as food or as labor-saving devices." Clearly there was no convincing him, for he claimed that God had revealed it all to him over coffee and raisin toast while he was reading his Bible. Well, maybe that's not *quite* the way he told it, but you understand what I was dealing with. This man, of course, didn't know he was walking in a mine field as we talked. I like it better when there's no warning.

After the fireworks, while the smoke was still clearing, I was tempted to put an end to his ranting by saying what I've said a hundred times before: "One of these days, I'm going to write something about the spiritual side of animals, and that will settle things." Except this time was different. As my stubborn friend declared that nothing in the world could convince him that animals had any spiritual value, I glanced at the thick script for this book, neatly stacked and almost ready to send to my publisher. It was a great moment. I smiled the secret smile of one who knows how God likes a challenge and said, "We'll see, my friend. We'll see."

—Susan DeVore Williams

CATS
The Love They Give Us

The Cat in the Conspiracy

by Aletha Lindstrom

*O*nly *eight o'clock and already this house is like an oven*, I thought irritably. Setting my coffee cup on the kitchen counter, I reached across the sink to close the shutters against the intense July heat. Just before they clicked shut, I glimpsed some small animal moving along a fence-row in the far pasture. A cat.

Another animal dumped, I decided—and felt a rush of anger at callous pet owners who abandon unwanted cats and dogs along country roads. But the incident was soon forgotten, swallowed by a deeper anger that had been seething inside me since an argument with my husband Andy the night before.

It was one of those times when he took charge of decision-making in a way that made me feel my own opinion and role in the matter were belittled. Or so it seemed to me. I'd responded sarcastically in a way well calculated to wound his pride. He'd made an angry reply. And so it built until we thoroughly disliked each other.

By bedtime we weren't speaking, and the silence continued through breakfast. I remembered the set look on his face as he shoved his chair away from the table, grabbed his briefcase and stalked silently out the door. Not one word of apology. Not even a *good-bye*.

This hadn't happened before in our 20 years of marriage. Like all husbands and wives, we exchanged occasional sharp words. But never had our anger lasted this long. And never had I felt so humiliated, so rejected. I refused to consider that Andy's usual good humor had been sabotaged by hot, sleepless nights—and by eight hours of daily sweltering in an office without air-conditioning. I refused to consider that I, too, was extremely edgy from a week of record-breaking temperatures.

Instead I nursed my grievance. "He'll probably come home expecting all to be forgiven and forgotten," I muttered. My bitter mood intensified as I cleared away coffee cups, untouched toast and bowls of half-eaten cereal. I lifted Andy's chair to replace it by the table. Suddenly I felt an urge to retaliate. "Well, it *won't* be forgotten! I'm tired of being treated like a child!" I slammed the chair down. "Maybe I won't even be here!" I said. "Let him find out how it feels to be walked out on!"

The boldness of the idea frightened me. Yet I felt determined— and strangely exhilarated. But where could I go? To relatives? To a motel? I'd have to think about it. Then some inner voice warned: *Get out of the house. Take a walk. Consider this carefully before you do something you'll regret!* I glanced at the clock. Eight-thirty. I still had plenty of time.

My energy, fueled by my need to get even, propelled me rapidly down the country road. The sun burned through my thin blouse, but I was more aware of the resentment simmering inside me. As I walked along, kicking angrily at stones, I dredged up old hurts and insults, building my case for leaving.

I'd covered about a half-mile when, for the first time, I noticed my surroundings. A farmhouse, vacant for several weeks, stood near the road. I often passed it when I drove into town. Now the dense shade of an ancient maple tree by the front porch proved irresistible.

I sank onto the bottom porch step and dropped my head to my arms. *If I'm going to get away by noon, I'd better get packed,* I thought.

Then I heard a faint, questioning "Meow?" and looked down to see a small white cat. Was it the animal I'd seen earlier along the fencerow? Probably. Foraging. By the looks of its emaciated little body, it hadn't had much success. For a moment I forgot my self-pity. "Why, you poor half-starved creature," I exclaimed. "I'll bet they moved out and left you!"

The scrawny kitten leaped on the step and tried to crawl into my lap. Instantly I regretted my words of concern. *I'll have trouble shaking her,* I thought in exasperation. I stood up and hurried out of the yard. But she came tumbling after me, crying, circling my feet, trying to rub against my legs.

I stopped. She sat down in front of me, looking up into my face. "Now, listen, cat," I said firmly. "We don't need a cat. I don't *want* a cat. So, scram! Get lost!" Her gaze never wavered.

I was about to pick her up and drop her over the fence into a cornfield when a large truck came bearing down on us, traveling much too fast for a country road. It thundered by, and when the dust cleared, the cat was gone, apparently terrified into headlong flight.

I walked back along the road, still brooding about leaving. Before I reached home, an idea came to me. We owned a cabin on a lake about four hours north. No telephone. No mail service. I'd just pack and go there. And I wouldn't leave a note for Andy. At first he'd think I'd gone on an errand. But when I hadn't returned by nightfall, he'd look in the bedroom closet and find my bag missing. He might do some calling around; then he'd probably conclude I'd gone to the cabin. But he wouldn't know for sure. He'd be angry—and he'd be worried. *Well, let him worry,* I thought grimly. *When he's concerned enough, he'll come after me. And he can apologize.*

I had nearly finished packing when that inner voice accosted me again: *What if he doesn't come after you? What if he won't apologize? He has a lot of pride, you know.*

Well, I was proud, too! Still, in spite of the heat, I felt a chill of apprehension. I couldn't recall ever going out, even on an errand, without leaving a note saying when I'd be back. And what if he didn't come after me? Would I come crawling home? Would this resentment remain, like an ugly, unhealing wound, between us? We loved each other deeply. But we had friends our age who'd loved each other, too, until an act of rejection, like the one I contemplated, became the first step toward separation—and eventual divorce.

Again I probed for the hurt inside me. It was still there. I felt my cheeks burn with anger, and the apprehension died. I zipped my bag firmly shut and hurried into the hall and out the back door.

My car, thank goodness, was filled with gas. I tossed my bag on the rear seat and backed out of the garage. Then I glanced at the seat beside me. The local newspaper I'd bought the day before lay there. By chance—or maybe it wasn't chance—I'd left it in the car when I'd carried the groceries into the house. Now one of the headlines on the front page caught my eye, "Boy Scouts Sponsor 'Be Kind to Animals' Program." *Be kind to animals.* The words seemed to leap out at me.

Animals? The cat! I'd completely forgotten her! Now the memory of the small helpless creature tugged at me. And for the second time that day I forgot my self-pity. How could I have been so heartless? ". . . *Inasmuch as ye have done it unto one of the least of these . . .*" (Matthew 25:40). Did God mean cats, too? I had no choice. I had to go back. And, remembering how the truck frightened her, I decided to walk.

"She's just a tramp," I told myself. "She'll be long gone by now—and I can leave with a clear conscience."

But she wasn't gone. When I approached the cornfield, she came bounding out, as if she'd been expecting me. And perhaps she had. She followed me home and into the kitchen.

I warmed milk for her and cut up some leftover chicken. "Go ahead, eat," I said, placing the food on the floor. I expected she'd gulp it ravenously like most hungry animals. I was wrong. As I turned to the refrigerator, I heard that same faint, questioning "Meow?" I looked down. She sat at my feet, her little face raised to mine.

"You've got food," I said in exasperation. "No self-respecting cat turns down chicken."

She raised a paw and timidly touched my leg. "Meow?" she cried again.

"What *is* it?" I said, picking her up. She nestled close to me, purring ecstatically, then rubbed her head against my cheek. Finally, she settled contentedly against my neck, singing that ridiculous little song.

So that was what she wanted! Love. Unbelievably, it was more important to that starving cat than food or drink. Love. The basic need of all God's creatures. Including me. *Including Andy,* I thought with a pang.

I placed the cat by her food and stroked her gently while she gobbled the chicken and lapped the milk. And I thought back through the previous afternoon and through the morning. That inner voice, the walk, the newspaper headline, the cat—all working together to keep me from leaving. Was it a conspiracy?

Suddenly I knew it was. God's conspiracy. Long ago I'd learned He sometimes uses unusual channels to save us from self-destruction.

I breathed a sigh of thanks. Then I remembered something I'd forgotten. No matter how good a marriage is, there are bound to be times of bitterness, of dissension, of wanting to "get even." The marriage vow is "for better, for worse," and we all need to build reserves of kindness and forgiveness to help us through the bad times. Because, as the little cat had just reminded me, love is by far the most important thing we have.

Stroking the soft fur, I searched once again for the angry resentment inside me. It was gone. The cat had finished eating, so I picked her up. Looking into her eyes, I said, "Andy doesn't like cats." She yawned, showing her pink little tongue. "But I love you," I added, "so he'll love you, too. He's that kind of guy."

Catalog

Cats sleep fat and walk thin.
Cats, when they sleep, slump;
When they wake, pull in—
And where the plump's been
There's skin.
Cats walk thin.
Cats wait in a lump,
Jump in a streak.
Cats, when they jump, are sleek
As a grape slipping its skin—
They have technique.
Oh, cats don't creak,
They sneak.

Cats sleep fat.
They spread comfort beneath them
Like a good mat,
As if they picked the place
And then sat.
You walk around one
As if he were the City Hall
After that.

If male,
A cat is apt to sing upon a minor scale:
This concert is for everybody, this
Is wholesale.
For a baton, he wields a tail.

(He is also found,
When he is happy, to resound
With an enclosed and private sound.)

A cat condenses.
He pulls in his tail to go under bridges,
And himself to go under fences.
Cats fit
In any size box or kit;
And if a large pumpkin grew under
one,
He could arch over it.

When everyone else is just ready to go
out,
The cat is just ready to come in.
He's not where he's been.
Cats sleep fat and walk thin.

—Rosalie Moore

Seeing-Eye Cats

by Brian McConnachie

In 1968 the Department of the Army began experimenting with the use of "night eyes," or seeing-eye cats. The Army had, for a long time, been quietly impressed with the night vision of cats. The mission of the project was to employ this special ability: harnessed cats were to lead foot-soldiers through the thick jungle during the dead of night.

After a month of night maneuvering with the seeing-eye cats, a report was filed with the section on Unconventional Warfare, which, in part, stated:

". . . A squad, upon being ordered to move out, was led off in all different directions by the cats.

". . . On many occasions the animals led the troops racing through thick brush in pursuit of field mice and birds.

". . . Troops had to force the cats to follow the direction of the patrol; the practice often led to the animals stalking and attacking the dangling pack straps of the American soldier marching directly in front of the animal.

". . . If the weather was inclement or even threatening inclemency, the cats were never anywhere to be found.

". . . Often when the troops were forced to take cover, the animals took the opportunity to sharpen their claws on the boots of the troops, regardless of the seriousness of the situation."

The project was suspended.

*Cats are a mys   nd of folk. There is more
passing in the   an we are aware of.*

—*Sir Walter Scott*

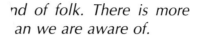

D r. Albert enowned
   scribble ine. The
because his aperb
Schweitzer   s left-handed, frequently
                        ons with his right hand
                        'ng on his left arm, and
                        b.

*God gave the cat to man so he might enjoy the
pleasure of caressing the tiger.*

—*Proverb*

*Cats know how to obtain food without labor, shelter
without confinement, and love without penalties.*

—*Walter Lionel George*

The smallest of felines is a masterpiece.

—Leonardo da Vinci

Cat Bathing as a Martial Art

by Bud Herron

Here are some tips on what to do when tabby starts smelling shabby.

Some people say cats never have to be bathed. They say cats lick themselves clean. They say cats have a special enzyme of some sort in their saliva that works like new, improved Wisk—dislodging the dirt where it hides and whisking it away.

I've spent most of my life believing this folklore. Like most blind believers, I've been able to discount all the facts to the contrary—the kitty odors that lurk in the corners of the garage and dirt smudges that cling to the throw rug by the fireplace.

The time comes, however, when a man must face reality; when he must look squarely in the face of massive public sentiment to the contrary and announce: "This cat smells like a port-a-potty on a hot day in Juarez."

When that day arrives at your house, as it has at mine, I have some advice you might consider as you place your feline friend under your arm and head for the bathtub:

—Know that cats are not reasonable creatures. Though you might want to sit down and discuss his odor eyeball-to-eyeball, don't expect him to understand. I have known only one or two cats in my entire life who could carry on a rational conversation and reach conclusions based on reasoning. If you tell the typical cat he stinks and therefore must have a bath, you will only warn him of his fate and make him that much more obstinate.

—Know that although the cat has the advantage of quickness and lack of concern for human life, you have the advantage of strength. Capitalize on that advantage by selecting the battlefield. Don't try to bathe him in an open area where he can force you to chase him. Pick a very small bathroom. If your bathroom is more than four feet square, I recommend that you get in the tub with the cat and close the sliding glass doors as if you were about to take a shower. (A simple shower curtain will not do. A berserk cat can shred a three-ply rubber shower curtain quicker than a politician can shift positions.)

—Know that a cat has claws and will not hesitate to remove all the skin from your body. Your advantage here is that you are smart and know how to dress to protect yourself. I recommend canvas overalls tucked into high-top construction boots, a pair of steel-mesh gloves, an army helmet, a hockey face mask, and a long-sleeve flak jacket.

—Prepare everything in advance. There is no time to go out for a towel when you have a cat digging a hole in your flak jacket. Draw the water. Make sure the bottle of kitty shampoo is inside the glass enclosure. Make sure the towel can be reached, even if you are lying on your back in the water.

—Use the element of surprise. Pick up your cat nonchalantly, as if to simply carry him to his supper dish. (Cats will not usually notice your strange attire. They have little or no interest in fashion as a rule. If he does notice your garb, calmly explain that you are taking part in a product-testing experiment for J.C. Penney.)

—Once you are inside the bathroom, speed is essential to survival. In a single liquid motion, shut the bathroom door, step into the tub enclosure, slide the glass door shut, dip the cat in the water, and squirt him with shampoo. You have now begun one of the wildest 45 seconds of your life. Cats have no handles. Add the fact that he now has soapy fur, and the problem is radically compounded. Do not expect to hold on to him for more than two or three seconds at a time. When you have him, however, you must remember to give him another squirt of shampoo and rub like crazy. He'll then spring free and fall back into the water, thereby rinsing himself off. (The national record is—for cats— three latherings, so don't expect too much.)

—Next, the cat must be dried. Novice bathers always assume this part will be the most difficult, for humans generally are worn out at this point and the cat is just getting really determined. In fact, the drying is simple compared to what you have just been through. That's because by now the cat is semipermanently affixed to your right leg. You simply pop the drain plug with your foot, reach for your towel, and wait. (Occasionally, however, the cat will end up clinging to the top of your army helmet. If this happens, the best thing to do is to shake him loose and to encourage him toward your leg.) After all the water is drained from the tub, it is a simple matter to just reach down and dry the cat.

In a few days the cat will relax enough to be removed from your leg. He will usually have nothing to say for about three weeks and will spend a lot of time sitting with his back to you. He might even become psychoceramic and develop the fixed stare of a plaster figurine.

You will be tempted to assume he is angry. This isn't usually the case. As a rule he is simply plotting ways to get through your defenses and injure you for life the next time you decide to give him a bath.

But if he is angry, what have you lost? If he is like most cats, he only tolerated you in the first place. Now at least he smells better while he abuses your hospitality.

We know that cats can climb down from trees without human assistance. After all, nobody has ever seen a cat skeleton in a tree.

—Author unknown

Portrait—8 Weeks

With paws that are petals
This tiger in brief
Is solemnly stalking
A flyaway leaf.
Enacting the hunt
On a miniature scale,
Distracted by shadows
And glimpses of tail,
Advancing, retreating,
With awkward good-will
In wide-eyed excitement,
And then strangely still,
For suddenly, softly,
And all in a heap,
The smallest of tigers
Has fallen asleep.

—Margaret Hillert

The Creatures

Rejoice in God, O ye Tongues; give the glory to the Lord,
    and the Lamb.
Nations, and languages, and every Creature in which is
    the breath of life.
Let man and beast appear before him, and magnify his
    name together.

—Christopher Smart, from *Jubilate Agno*

Pangur Ban

I and Pangur Ban, my cat,
'Tis a like task we are at;
Hunting mice is his delight,
Hunting words I sit all night.

Oftentimes a mouse will stray
In the hero Pangur's way;
Oftentimes my keen thought set
Takes a meaning in its net.

When a mouse darts from its den,
Oh, how glad is Pangur then!
Oh, what gladness do I prove
When I solve the doubts I love!

So in peace our task we ply,
Pangur Ban—my cat—and I;
In our arts we find our bliss,
I have mine and he has his.

—Anonymous 9th-century Irish monk

Pat Boone and Family Cat, Ariel

I've always loved cats. Growing up in Nashville, we once had as many as seventeen cats at a time, with kittens on the way! We bought Ariel for our daughter Debby when she was a teenager and Ariel was a little Persian kitten. Until Debby left home to be married, he was her own cat—but Debby left him behind when she went with her husband, Gabriel. So we've loved Ariel even more than any other cat, and he is special.

Our pets are our friends, truly members of our family, and we have prayed for them when they were sick, just like we would any other member of our family. And God has answered our prayers many times, more than once miraculously! Since He created animals even before He created man and woman, we believe that all animals are special to Him—and therefore, even more special to us.

—Pat Boone

A Candle for Samantha

by Catherine Vanicek

Samantha came to us on a crisp, late autumn day. We took her in, my family and I, and soon that skinny, flea-ridden kitten rewarded us by turning into as gentle and loving a friend as we ever could have wished. That was the first year.

The second year found Samantha completely grown. With the typical ingenuity of the household cat, she invented many of her own diversions. She discovered that eating from the dog's bowl was a surefire way to initiate an invigorating game of chase and that riding home from the veterinarian's office resulted in a pretty special meal if she could manage to look sufficiently emotionally bruised. And when she'd been an especially good kitty she could—oh, so rarely!—coax her people to supply her with a great smelling pine tree covered with plastic bells for her to bat about. All in all, it was not a bad life. Who could have predicted that in her third year, things could go so wrong?

To this day we do not understand how she got out of the house. We simply know that she accomplished it. As weather stations reported a chilling frost, my children and I took to the streets with our photos of Sam. House after house turned us away; field after frozen field yielded no hope. But we did not give up.

Early on the second day, we began our search anew, driven by predictions of possible snow. My daughter Camberley, too distraught to attend school, helped me tape posters in windows and check out our local animal control shelter. Knowing that pets are inclined to playfully follow groups of children, we called in an announcement to local schools and asked that it be publicized on their public address systems. We followed that up by sifting through newspaper lost-and-found columns. Then, after exhausting all the ideas at our disposal, we once more searched door to door, calling aloud for the homeless waif who, until then, had been warm, sheltered, and loved. She had been warm and therefore lacked the heavy winter coat needed to survive extended freezing temperatures; sheltered, but now without protecting walls; loved, yet now alone.

Then, mercilessly, the storm broke, bringing with it high winds, drifting snow, and single-digit temperatures. Camberley cried herself to sleep that night. Michael holed up in his room and stared stoically at the raging weather outside his window.

Samantha's face haunted all of us with the plethora of "if onlys": If only we had seen her sneak out and had stopped her; if only we lived in an area where cat licensing was mandatory; if only we had provided her with an identification tag, so that we could be notified were she found alive—or dead. No news is good news, the saying goes, but not when the life of your valued pet is at stake—not when you are missing a friend.

Then, on the third night, came an inspiration: *A candle in the window.* In days gone by, women placed a single candle in the window to welcome passersby, or to reach out and greet homecoming family members in the dark of night. Samantha would be terribly cold, but if she were nearby, lights might entice her home. They would suggest warmth and perhaps draw her like a moth is drawn to a flame.

Rushing to the family room, I flung the drapes wide and flooded the area with welcoming light, watching with desperate anticipation as the glow spilled out invitingly upon frigid snow. Next, from the cupboard, I secured a bowl and filled it with a can of tuna—people-style. Sam would love that! She was cold, yes, but she would be hungry, too—ravenous if I were lucky. A temptingly pungent bowl of tuna would be difficult to pass up after three days in the snow.

After turning the heat up to 80 degrees, I opened the sliding glass doors just wide enough to admit a lonely waif from the freezing night, and placed the bowl of tuna on the floor, well into the light. Then, heedless of the sleep of family members and neighbors, I gave out a shrill, high-pitched cat call, left the room, and turned off every other light in the house. I had thought like a cat. If that didn't work, there would be nothing else left to try.

The next morning, after three hours of restless sleep, I

awakened to the sight of yet another slate gray, snow-filled sky. Dreading what I would find, but unable to stay away any longer, I crept cautiously into the family room. There in the middle of the sofa, deeply burrowed into the comforting warmth of her favorite fuzzy afghan, was the thin form of our beloved tortoise shell cat. Her plate was empty, and she was sound asleep.

Our story, fortunately, had a happy ending: Samantha survived. She hugged the heater for days, leaving its warmth only to relieve hunger and thirst, but she came back to us in fair health, considering what she had been through. Now when the last leaves of summer swirl away on the breath of a of a frigid fall, when snow clouds threaten the security of our small town, I pick up my cat and hold her close. And as my mind wanders back to that other day and that other time, I give special thanks for the inspiration of a candle for Samantha.

Night Cat

That sly old sky-eyed cat, all camouflaged for night
Picking through twig and stem, soundlessly stalks
A shadow's flying form,
And on her clandestine mission hums a tune
No human ear has heard.

—Susan DeVore Williams

S ir Winston Churchill, a prime minister of England and one
of the century's greatest statesmen, ate his meals at home
with Jock, a ginger cat. He refused to begin eating until his
servants had brought the pet to the table.

"P uss," presumed to be the oldest cat who ever lived,
died in Devonshire, England, at the age of thirty-six.
Another Devonshire cat allegedly lived to age thirty-four.

Cat's Attention Span

by Stephen Baker

Activity	*Attention Span*
Being called	2 seconds
Being called by name	2 seconds
Being told to go somewhere else	None
Being told to go somewhere else in a loud voice	None
Smelling filet of sole wafting across living room	Half hour
Dog barking	5 seconds
Dog barking at the cat	2 seconds
Owner unmaking bed to retire	10 minutes
Birds outside the window	1 hour
Pat on the back	2 seconds
Scratching between the ears	5 hours
Half-hour TV program	Half hour (minus commercials)
Owner unpacking groceries	10 minutes
Owner putting food in refrigerator	10 minutes
Owner getting out of bed in the morning before cat does	None
Owner leaving home	1 second
Owner returning home with bag of groceries	15 seconds

The Box

by Mary Louise Kitsen

There's more to do than I can handle," I said loudly and clearly. Of course, there was no one to hear my complaint except the three cats lying on the bed. Two of them continued sleeping while the third laid her ears back and switched her tail.

I sighed. There were writing assignments to be done (I'm a full-time free-lance writer), my cousins were coming from Kansas in a few days, and I felt I had to clean the entire house. And my mother was in the hospital again, which meant two trips there each day. How would I get to everything?

Deciding that Jesus was the only One Who was listening, I addressed Him directly this time. "With Your help, I'll make it, but please, don't let anything else happen right now."

It was still early in the morning. I slipped my robe on and started downstairs. Maybe if I relaxed briefly with some toast and coffee, taking a look at the morning paper at the same time, I'd feel ready to tackle the busy day ahead. I opened the door and picked up the newspaper. Then I saw the box.

Where did it come from? It was a large box with "Corn Flakes" written on the side. An old, rusted window screen lay on top; a rope kept it in place. Oh, no . . . someone who knows how I feel about cats must have dumped some kittens on me again. Just what I needed!

I started to pick the box up, and when I felt how heavy it was, I thought, "They've dumped the mother cat too." Actually, I didn't know the half of it!

I set the box down in the living room, untied the rope and looked in. There was a big yellow cat. But where were her kittens? I reached in and lifted the cat out. It started to purr immediately and pushed its head tightly against my shoulder. One big cat? A male cat at that.

I held the cat up to take a better look at him. And started to sob.

This big, beautiful cat had no eyes—just white skin where his eyes should have been. I cradled him as my other cats started to gather. Pip-Squeak rubbed against the newcomer with evident pleasure. But what was I going to do with a blind kitty? How much care would he need?

I looked in the box to see if there was anything else and found the note: "This is Poppy. My dad hates having him around and said he'd shoot him if Mom and I didn't get rid of him ourselves. Please take care of him." It was in the handwriting of a youngster. Poor, sad child trying to keep a blind cat alive.

Poppy ate with the other cats—to my surprise and relief—and I showed him the litter box. I got absolutely nothing done before it was time to leave for the hospital; and I worried about leaving the cat in a strange place. But he seemed content and interested in investigating things. I called the vet's office and made an appointment. Then I left, praying that Poppy would make out all right.

When I returned home, I found Poppy sleeping with Pip-Squeak in the sunny dining room window. In the early afternoon I put him in a carrier and headed for the vet's office. I hated to take him, but I had to have help in this matter. The vet took him into a back room to check him over. I sat straight as a pin, not knowing what to expect.

The vet finally came out. He was alone. My heart did a flip-flop. What about Poppy? At that moment I realized the big yellow cat had stolen my heart.

"Someone took good care of that fellow," the doctor told me. "He's in good shape and amazingly contented. We'll keep him a couple days. He should be altered and have some shots, and there are a few tests we'd like to do."

I grinned.

Then the bomb fell. "We think Poppy is deaf and dumb as well as blind."

For the next two days I wondered how I'd manage a pet that couldn't see, hear or make a sound. I prayed about the cat. And, to my surprise, I was getting an awful lot of things accomplished even though my mind stayed on Poppy. It was as though Poppy was a challenge and so everything else was a challenge too.

I brought Poppy and my mother home from their respective hospitals just two days later. I went for Mom first and got her settled in her favorite chair in the living room. Then I went for Poppy.

Mom moved to the edge of her chair as I brought the carrier in. I opened it, and Poppy climbed into my arms. How he loved people! I carried him over to Mom, and she gathered him to her. In minutes, Poppy purred happily on her lap. It was the start of a warm, personal friendship between an elderly lady and a handicapped kitty cat—a relationship that made both of their lives happier.

Poppy had helped me too. I was feeling sorry for myself when he came, but through him I gained a better attitude. It seemed almost as if Jesus had helped guide Poppy's owners to the act of bringing him to me. Little by little I began to think more and more about the mother and child who had left Poppy in my care. Who were they? Would they wonder about what had happened to Poppy?

And then one day I made a sign that said "Poppy is fine" and taped it to my front porch. I hoped the youngster who had brought the cat to me would see it.

The sign stayed up for several days. Then came the morning I went outside to the garage and I saw something that made life even better. Written on the bottom of the sign I'd made were two messages, evidently written by the child and his mother—or that's what I've always thought. The child's writing said, "Thank you." The adult's hand wrote, "God bless you."

Thy righteousness is like the great mountains; thy judg-
ments are a great deep: O Lord, thou preservest man and
beast.

—Psalms 36:6

*The playful kitten with its pretty little tigerish gambol
is infinitely more amusing than half the people one
is obliged to live with in the world.*

—Lady Sydney Morgan

Here Among the Daffodils

Here among the daffodils
Walks a golden tiger cat.
Where the golden sunlight spills
Softly through the daffodils
Treads a golden acrobat.

And the blossoms lifting up
Frame a pansy face of fur.
Near each perfect flower cup,

Golden paws are lifted up.
Softly golden is the purr.

Cat and flowers shine with light
While the tiger reigns supreme,
Tail among the stems upright
And the golden eyes alight
With a golden-flowered dream.

—Margaret Hillert

She Sights a Bird

She sights a Bird—she chuckles—
She flattens—then she crawls—
She runs without the look of feet—
Her eyes increase to Balls—

Her Jaws stir—twitching—hungry—
Her Teeth can hardly stand—

She leaps, but Robin leaped the first—
Ah, Pussy, of the Sand,

The Hopes so juicy ripening—
You almost bathed your Tongue—
When Bliss disclosed a hundred
  Toes—
And fled with every one—

—Emily Dickinson

My Cat

My pretty cat to my heart I hold,
My heart ever warm to her;
Let me look in thine eyes of agate and gold;
Thy claws keep sheathed in fur.

—Charles Baudelaire

Learn the Cat Language

by Dr. Michael W. Fox

Cats behave in various ways to tell you how they feel and what they want. I call this "Felinese," the cat language. Learn to interpret cats' signals of communication, and you'll better understand cats. You may even surprise your cat-owning friends, who may never have heard of Felinese.

When a cat looks at you and then half closes its eyes, it's not ignoring you. The animal is telling you that it's relaxed in your presence. A scared cat would stare at you and hiss, or run away if you moved toward it. And you would see the pupils of its eyes dilate, a clear sign of fear.

When you approach a friendly cat, extend one fingertip slowly to touch its nose. The cat will put its nose out to touch your finger very briefly. Cats touch each other's noses this way as a friendly signal, like people shaking hands.

Cats have special scent glands on their foreheads, lips, and tails which they use to mark their territory and their friends. They will rub their foreheads and lips against each other, against you, and perhaps against furniture in your house. Cats seem to use their body scent as a marker to make them feel secure and connected with each other.

Many adult cats, when being petted, will drool and push against you just as though they were a nursing kitten. This is natural. It's their way of saying, "I love and trust you so much that I can be a kitten in your arms."

Often, when a cat is being stroked, it will lift its tail and hindquarters straight up in the air. Cats use this tail "semaphore" signal for the same reason a dog wags its tail—to show friendliness.

Cats lash their tails from side to side when they are excited or angry. When they're afraid, they fluff out their tails, which makes them seem larger than usual. They will often arch their backs to make themselves look even bigger, and they might unleash a scary scream to frighten a rival.

When a cat wants to play, it will look at you and then flop over onto one side. This is an invitation to gently wrestle the cat, which will fight back playfully with soft, mild bites and scratches. To show submission, a cat will simply remain still, in a crouched position.

All cats purr, but some purr so quietly you can hardly hear them. They purr to signal a relaxed, friendly mood. And their purring may also help relax them and those around them who feel and hear their purring—like getting a nice massage in sound.

When a meow is combined with a purr, the cat may be saying "I want . . ." (meow) "something pleasant" (purr). Hence, many cats will give a purr-meow-purr when they want to be fed or petted.

Cat "talk" mimics our own, at least in tone. The tone of a cat's various sounds tells a lot about the animal's feelings, just as tone of voice shows our own feelings. A plaintive meow signals loneliness; a scream means fear; a growl or threatening hiss shows anger. So it's not surprising that cats, like other animals, can tell what we are feeling when we speak in a soft, friendly, purring voice or in a growling, angry one.

Cats are like us in other ways, too. Sometimes they become depressed, looking sad and sitting alone. I've seen cats get depressed when a companion cat or dog in their house died or when they were left in a boarding kennel by owners going on vacation.

Some cats are shy of strangers and run to hide when visitors come. Others like to be the center of attention, parading through a room with tail in the air, rubbing their heads and legs against visitors.

Now you know some of the ways in which cats communicate with you. Technically speaking, this is called *ethology*, the study of animal behavior. But we can call it Felinese. The more you understand Felinese, the more you will recognize what different personalities different cats have.

Most importantly, you can recognize that cats are sensitive and intelligent creatures who deserve our respect. They can communicate very well with each other and with us, if we take time out to observe and learn from them.

Dr. Michael W. Fox is the Scientific Director of the Humane Society of the United States. This article appeared in his column in Boy's Life *magazine.*

Body Language

by Lesley Sussman and Sally Bordwell

Cats have a unique vocabulary of movement. The swishing of the tail can indicate anger. A tail held high and straight usually indicates pleasure and happiness. There are many such gestures through which your feline companion tries to communicate with you. So the next time you're trying to figure out what's on Tabby's mind, ask him. If you get no verbal reply, pay attention to his movements and consult this chart.

1. Licking your hand or fingers: A gesture of love (or you've dipped your fingers in the tuna salad).
2. Rhythmic, horizontal lashing of the tail: Anger.
3. Ears folded down flat: Greater anger—watch out!
4. Tail and coat fluff up: Usually occurs in the presence of another animal. Indicates anger.
5. Tail high and straight: Pleasure and happiness.
6. Tail drooping: Disappointment.
7. Whiskers drooping: Bored.
8. Whiskers pressed flat against the muzzle: Contentment.
9. Squeezing of eyes: Happy and relaxed. Sign of affection.
10. Purring and gently waving tail: Contentment.
11. Patting body with a paw: Sharing.
12. Head snuggled against body, tail high: Trust and affection.

THE CAT'S ANGRY FACES

During an aggressive encounter the pupils of the eye, the angle of the ears, and the raising of the fur are clues to what the cat is feeling.

"All's well."	"I'm alarmed."	"I'm going to attack."
"But maybe I won't."	"I warn you . . ."	". . . I'll swat!"
"I warn you, I'll bite."	"Keep your distance . . ."	". . .or else!!"

From HOW TO TALK TO YOUR ANIMALS, copyright © 1985 by Jean Craighead George. Reproduced by permission of Harcourt Brace Jovanovich, Inc.

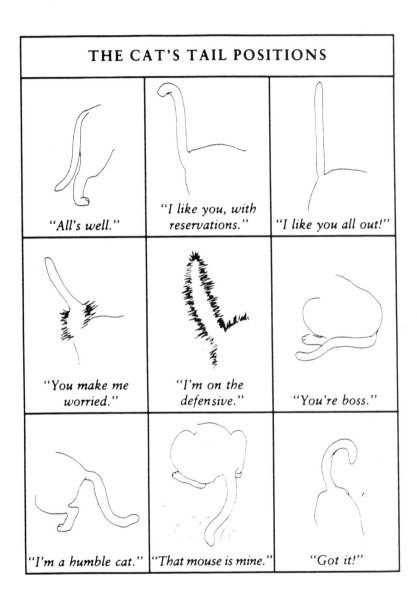

THE CAT'S TAIL POSITIONS

"All's well."

"I like you, with reservations."

"I like you all out!"

"You make me worried."

"I'm on the defensive."

"You're boss."

"I'm a humble cat."

"That mouse is mine."

"Got it!"

From HOW TO TALK TO YOUR ANIMALS, copyright © 1985 by Jean Craighead George. Reproduced by permission of Harcourt Brace Jovanovich, Inc.

Personal Thoughts About Animals

by C. S. Lewis

Can We Love Animals Too Much?

August 18, 1956

Dear Mary,

. . . I will never laugh at anyone for grieving over a loved beast. I think God wants us to love Him *more*, not to love creatures (even animals) *less*. We love everything in *one* way too much (i.e. at the expense of our love for Him) but in another way we love everything too little.

No person, animal, flower, or even pebble has ever been loved too much—i.e. more than every one of God's works deserves. But you need not feel "like a murderer" [to have euthanized a suffering pet]. Rather rejoice that God's law allows you to extend to Fanda that last mercy which (no doubt, quite rightly) we are forbidden to extend to suffering humans. You'll get over this. . . .

God bless you—and Fanda!

About Cats:

October 2, 1962

Dear Mary,

. . . I am glad to hear you have rehabilitated a displaced cat. I can't understand the people who say cats are not affectionate. Our Siamese (my "step-cat") is almost suffocatingly so. True, our ginger Tom (a great Don Juan and a mighty hunter before the Lord) will take no notice of *me*, but he will of others. He thinks I'm not quite socially up to his standards, and makes this very clear. No creature can give such a crushing "snub" as a cat! He sometimes looks at the dog—a big Boxer puppy, very anxious to be friendly—in a way that makes it want to sink to the floor. . . .

Will Animals Be Part of the Resurrection?

November 26, 1962

Dear Mary,

. . . My stuff about animals came long ago in *The Problem of Pain*.* I ventured the supposal—it could be nothing more—that as we are raised *in* Christ, so at least some animals are raised *in* us. Who knows, indeed, but that a great deal even of the inanimate creation is raised *in* the redeemed souls who have, during this life, taken its beauty into themselves? That may be the way the "new heaven and the new earth" are formed. Of course we can only guess and wonder. But these particular guesses arise in me, I trust, from taking seriously the resurrection of the body: a doctrine which now-a-days is very soft pedalled by nearly all the faithful—to our great impoverishment.

From *Letters to an American Lady*

---

*Refers to Lewis' best-selling book, *The Problem of Pain,* available from your local bookstore or from Macmillan Publishing Company,

A Cat by Any Other Name . . .

The most popular names for cats, according to a survey of some 7,000 cat owners by Anderson Animal Shelter of South Elgin, Illinois:

1. Sam or Samantha
2. Kitty
3. Tiger
4. Boots
5. Princess
6. Patches
7. Muffin or Muffy
8. Smokey
9. Fluffy
10. Tom

More than half the cats in the survey had "people names." The most popular seemed to be Clyde, Oscar, Tiffany, Max, Cindy. A fair number were named for favorite television, movie, or cartoon characters—Morris, Garfield, E.T., Pebbles, Tattoo, Yoda, and Mr. T, for example. One was named simply TV.

Preppy names like Buffy, Muffy, Sissy, Missy, and Fluffy raised the list to the level of an Eastern girls' school's sorority roster.

Dozens of cats were simply named Kitty or Cat.

Many had names that enticed prospective adoptees: Snuggles, Mellow, Happy, Cutie. Some, however, had names that put them

at a disadvantage—Puddles, Sneaky, Digger, Mischief, and Sassy. Others apparently reminded their owners of memorable dates or places. One was named February 14, and others were called Kansas, Aspen, Reno, and Skokie.

Nobody explained the significance of the name given to Foggy Bottom, a tortoiseshell cat.

King Henry II, who mercilessly persecuted the Protestants in France, often fell over in a dead faint at the sight of a cat.

If man could be crossed with a cat, it would improve man, but it would deteriorate the cat.

—*Mark Twain*

Curiosity killed the cat, satisfaction brought it back.

—*Wise Old Saying*

Cat Jeoffry

For I will consider my Cat Jeoffry.
For he is the servant of the Living God, duly and daily serving
  him.
For at the first glance of the glory in the East he worships in his
  way.
For this is done by wreathing his body seven times round with
  elegant quickness.
For then he leaps up to catch the musk, which is the blessing of
  God upon his prayer.
. . . For when his day's work is done his business more properly
  begins.
For he keeps the Lord's watch in the night against the
  adversary.
For he counteracts the powers of darkness by his electrical skin
  and glaring eyes.
For he counteracts the Devil, who is death, by brisking about the
  life.
. . . For he is of the tribe of Tiger.
For the Cherub Cat is a term of the Angel Tiger.
. . . For he purrs in thankfulness, when God tells him he's a good
  cat.
For he is an instrument for the children to learn benevolence
  upon.
For every house is incompleat without him and a blessing is
  lacking in spirit.
For the Lord commanded Moses concerning the cats at the
  departure of the Children of Israel from Egypt.
For every family had one cat at least in the bag.
. . . For he is tenacious of his point.
For he is a mixture of gravity and waggery.
For he knows that God is his Savior.
For there is nothing sweeter than his peace when at rest.
For there is nothing brisker than his life when in motion.

For the divine spirit comes about his body to sustain it in
   compleat cat.

. . . For he can fetch and carry, which is patience in employment.

For he can jump over a stick which is patience upon proof
   positive.

For he can spraggle upon waggle at the word of command.

For he can jump from an eminence into his master's bosom.

For he can catch the cork and toss it again.

For he is hated by the hypocrite and miser.

For the former is afraid of detection.

For the latter refuses the charge.

. . . For he is good to think on, if a man would express himself
   neatly.

. . . For God has blessed him in the variety of his movements.

For, tho' he cannot fly, he is an excellent clamberer.

For his motions upon the earth are more than any other
   quadrupede.

For he can tread to all the measures upon the musick.

For he can swim for life.

For he can creep.

—Christopher Smart

Sweet Sam, Farewell

by Patty Cormaney

Around Sam's neck I fastened his little blue leather collar with its silver heart engraved with his name and address in case we lost him.

Around his thinning body I wrapped his little blue blanket, and then Sam and I sat together in the van while Elmer went in to see the veterinarian.

And then Elmer came to the door and beckoned. I carried Sam through the office into an examination room. All the time the tears were running down my face so that I could scarcely see. Elmer took Sam in his arms and the kindly veterinarian took me in his own. I cried all over his starched white coat.

Sam was crying, too. Then I went out the door and Elmer held Sam in his arms until he died.

We buried Sam behind the veterinary clinic, and we bought cement to make a gravestone. Then we drove away from the town more than a thousand miles from home and that was the end of 19 years of traveling with Samovar, the perfect Persian cat.

From the beginning we'd been warned against him.

"Take that kitten back where you bought him," said the veterinarian who examined him. "He has pneumonia, and he won't live long."

What none of us knew then was that he'd also fall prey to chronic kidney stones and we'd have to struggle with that problem all across the map.

But we looked down at the kitten that first day and our hearts melted. We didn't have children, and this was an orphan who was in desperate need of a home. He was so small I could hold him in the palm of one hand. My sister told me never to punish him. "It would be like spanking a mouse," she sighed.

So that's how Sam came to be a member of our family and how I began to include him in the often hilarious crises of our trailer travels. Articles about Sam appeared in several publications and eventually in this magazine. He may not have known he was a rather famous cat, but he did know how smart he was. He also felt he was not only special but beautiful. We thought so, too.

As the years passed, Sam developed arthritis. Then it became more difficult for him to chew. So I bought baby food by the case, causing supermarket checkers to do double takes as they noted I appeared a little old for infant motherhood.

On one of our last trips, though, Sam lost his appetite. He lost interest in all the passing parade from the trailer's one-way windows. He no longer felt like taking a walk for the arthritis was painful.

When we knew at last that there was no alternative, Elmer and I found a compassionate doctor and a quiet resting place for Sam.

In *Trailer Life's Mail Box* I read the continuing controversy between pet owners in trailer parks and other residents who resent the thoughtlessness and improper care of animals exhibited by some who travel with their dogs or cats. I can understand both sides. Sam did, too. He hated noisy pet areas and considered a sandbox the only proper facility when needed.

He was an elegant old gentleman, our Sam. In human years, he was about 133, and that should be enough to satisfy anybody. Anybody, that is, except a courageous cat who seemed almost human and two humans who married too late to start a family and settled for a pet.

Sam loved the trailer, and he also loved us with his tired heart. For such a little fellow, he gave us enormous pleasure every day of his life.

Sleep well, sweet Sam. Some day may your heaven also be our own.

—From "Uneasy Rider,"
a column in *Trailer Life*
magazine

For a Very Old Cat

Living, I cannot think you dead,
    And the soft purr stilled forever in
    your throat.
My fingers grip your bony head,
    Trace hard against the pattern of
    your coat,
Grasp firm a fold of aging flesh.
Your fur smells sweet and fresh.

You welcome my attentions, close
    And open wide your paws in ancient
    rite.
The orange triangle of your nose
    Touches me damply. Your old eyes
    light

With vestiges of former flame.
I gently say your name.

And there are those who will won-
    der why
    Such feeling should exist for a
    dumb beast.
But others, kin to earth and sky,
    Who talk to trees, stargaze, and
    call the least
Small flower by name, find ample
    traces
That love has many faces.

—Margaret Hillert

A cat is a lion in a jungle of bushes.
                                —Proverb

C ardinal Richelieu kept a beautifully furnished room for his cats. Caretakers were charged with feeding them chicken patés twice daily. When the cardinal died the cats and caretakers were generously provided for in his will.

W hen I play with my cat, who knows whether she is not amusing herself with me more than I with her?

                                —Montaigne

T he cat is the companion of the fireside.

                                —Edward E. Whiting

Stray

Out on the walk he sat,
All cat,
Bristling fierce inside his fur,
Unsure,
Sporting a tattered ear,

The fear
Of past rejections plain,
And pain.
But at one gentle word
(Spoken in love)
He purred.

—Margaret Hillert

There are an estimated 75 million cats in the United States. Unfortunately, about 15 to 18 million of them are strays which must live off the land and survive as best they can. A stray's life span is extremely short.

Kitty Love

by Patty Cormaney

He was so black that at night you couldn't even see what he was unless he happened to be standing on the picnic table, silhouetted against the side of the trailer.

What he was, was a plain old black cat. Everybody in the park called him Midnight. I just settled for Kitty.

I'd have settled for any kitty at all. We'd had Samovar, our 19-year-old Persian, put to sleep several months before and were on a trip to forget. The park we picked was lovely. Tall trees gave us shade. Water lapped at the lip of the boat dock. The recreation center was as handsome as all those improbable photos, except this one was real. Who could ask for anything more?

Anything more turned out to be Kitty, the park cat.

The people who'd just left our space had recently suffered the death of their own black cat. They tried to adopt Kitty in a misguided effort that nearly wrecked their tow vehicle. On a trial run, Kitty let them know he wasn't about to go bye-bye with anybody. He knew when he had it made, and that didn't entail a trip to anywhere else. I assume they'd had their upholstery replaced by now.

But they'd been feeding Kitty, so he was primed for the next occupants by the time we pulled in. He wasn't about to let a good thing end. Somehow he knew we were an easy mark, and he fell heir to all the gourmet goodies we'd had on hand for Sam. Kitty dined on roast beef, fish, and baby food. He lapped up evaporated milk.

The park manager strolled over. "I wish you'd quit feeding that cat," he said. "When you leave, he'll just hang around waiting for food."

Guilt turned my face as red as Kitty was black. One of the park regulars took me aside. "That cat will never go hungry," he said. "Everybody in this park has been feeding him all along."

Kitty trotted right back to our door, looking like the cat that ate the canary, which is about the only delicacy with which we didn't provide him. Every morning he sat on the trailer step waiting for the door to open. I nearly mashed him flat a couple of times before learning to step out cautiously.

Kitty had adopted us as obviously as we'd adopted him, even though we knew this relationship couldn't last forever. Our own upholstery would never stand up to cat claws, and Kitty's happy home wasn't ours. We're more a pair of strays than he was.

Finally, though, we had to head home. The day before, we took a box of dry cat food and plastic dishes to another camper on Kitty's sucker list. He promised to do unto Kitty as lavishly as we had done.

Next morning we had already hooked up the trailer and checked the trailer lights and brakes by the time Kitty showed up for breakfast. As usual, he was doing his drum-major high step through the grass, purring for all he was worth and weaving an invisible rug around our ankles.

It was like saying good-bye all over again. Sam had been the crème de la crème of Persians, and Kitty was a far meow from purebred. But I felt again the pangs of farewell as I parceled out a precious turkey breast.

Once more I was surreptitiously wiping away a tear or two as Elmer cleared his throat and the traffic. We still miss our Sam most of all, but now and then we remember Kitty who, all unknowingly, helped us over a hurdle or two when we needed him even more than he needed us.

Even now sometimes I paraphrase the old song and think of Kitty: Oh, I wonder who's feeding him now? I wonder who's hearing him meow.

From "Uneasy Rider,"
Trailer Life magazine

Application

Ahem!
I am available.
I have no home,
No friends,
And no immediate prospects.

Not to give you a hardluck story,
But things have not been going so well
    with me lately.
I had a nice family
But the old lady died
And the man hated cats
So out I went.

You can see I know how to look after myself,
Though I don't know for how much longer
In a filthy street
And no decent place to clean up.
I've been used to good things.

Housebroken? Of course,
Completely.
I am rather loyal.
I would be your cat—
Show it, I mean
When people come to visit,
By making a fuss over you,
And responding when you called me.

I'm not too finicky about food,
Food! Oh dear!
My stomach is empty
And my heart is desolate.

I'm not meant to be a street cat,
Or make myself a furtive shadow
In an alley.
I'm lonely, lonely, lonely,
And frightened!
Please may I come in?

—Paul Gallico

A Counseling Psychologist Answers the Questions Families Ask Most About Pets

by Rebecca L. True

REBECCA TRUE, R.N., M.A., M.F.C.C., spent a number of years as a pediatric nurse, gaining extensive experience with critically and chronically ill children and grieving families. She now does marriage, family, and child counseling. With her husband, a psychiatrist, she has for several years practiced with a group of Christian counselors in Northern California.

What are some of the psychological benefits pets can offer to families?

One of the best things animals can do is to help families learn about relationships. Starting very early, kids can begin to expand their awareness of the world beyond their own family through books and stories about pets. Later, as they gain experience with real-life pets, kids can learn valuable lessons about love, empathy, and even about loss and grief. Of course, they can also learn about sex and procreation by observing animals during pregnancy and when they give birth. Even if the family's own pets don't have babies, kids can be taken to zoos, kennels, farms, or to a neighbor's house to watch the birth process. These experiences are ideal opportunities for families to talk openly about reproduction.

Pets also are ideal examples for children. They give unconditional love—something we very rarely (if ever) experience in human relationships. It's easier for kids to understand the unconditional love of God if they can sample a bit of that kind of love from a dog or cat. Even parents who love their children very deeply tend to attach conditions to their love without realizing it. As a result, it's possible for a child to grow up without knowing what it's like to be loved exactly the way he is—even at his very worst—without being rejected, betrayed, belittled, or shamed for "falling short." Dogs and cats are especially good at giving children that kind of experience. Kids quickly learn that they can tell their pets the secret thoughts that no one else can be trusted with. Animals are there to comfort and to share the important moments in life. Friends may walk away in the middle of a crisis, but the dog or cat will stay by your side as long as it's needed. A pet neither lectures nor admonishes; it simply listens, responds, and comforts in a thoroughly satisfying way.

Animals also can teach lessons about life in the real world. For example, when you're trying to explain to a child the difference between "safe" and "unsafe" people—those who can and can't be trusted—the child will understand much more easily if you explain in terms of animals. You can say, "We trust our own dog because we know her so well. We know what she'll do if we pet her and play with her. But we never approach or try to touch a dog we don't know, because that dog might bite. It might seem friendly, but until we've known that dog for a long time we don't trust it to come near enough to hurt us." This kind of example often brings home a vital message that would otherwise not get through. These lessons carry through to the child's relationships with people, too.

Children today spend much more time alone than they did in the days when most moms stayed at home to take care of them. Now, the family home can be a lonely, frightening place for "latch-key" kids who let themselves into an empty house to wait for parents, brothers, or sisters to get home. Pets can make "goin' home time" a much happier prospect for these youngsters. A friendly wag or a warm purr can say "welcome home" in just the way a child needs to hear it. Pets are also good for kids experiencing other kinds of loneliness—divorce, a new baby brother or sister, or a death in the family, for example. In times like that, it's reassuring to have a loving relationship that's predictable and unchanging.

How can parents know when their children are ready for a pet, and how can they choose a pet that will be ideal for their family?

First, I think it's important to avoid impulsive pet ownership. It's amazing how many people get a pet simply because their kids bring one home, or they see a cute puppy or kitten in a shop window and buy it on the spur of the moment. Parents who want to avoid problems should never get a family pet without preparing for it over time.

It's always wise to have a "waiting period" before bringing a pet into the family. No matter how children may beg, cry, pout, or plead, it's important to be sure the child is really ready for the responsibilities a pet will involve. Every child will promise to take care of the new pet, but remember, kids aren't born understanding what it means to have an animal's life and welfare depend on them.

During the waiting period—which should be at least a month, but ideally would be much longer—the family can talk together about what sort of pet would be happiest in their household. Some questions they could discuss might be:

   —What do we expect a pet to do for us—individually and
      as a family? Children should talk about why they want
      the particular pet they have in mind. Parents can gain
      new insights into the needs of their children and steer
      them toward appropriate pets.
   —How will a pet fit into the framework of our daily life?
   —What activities are we involved in that can include the
      pet?
   —Will we want the pet in the house most of the time, or
      outside? Dogs especially need large doses of human
      companionship to be happy. Nothing is more miserable
      than an "outside dog" who spends his days longing for
      the company of owners whose lives are too busy to
      devote a few hours a day to him. Active families that
      can't spend time with a dog should opt for a cat, a bird,
      or another more independent creature that won't suffer
      as much from loneliness.
   —How much time will each of us realistically want to
      spend feeding, training, grooming, and playing with a

pet? If this will be a family pet (as opposed to little Jennifer's or Bobby's pet), parents need to decide how much responsibility they're willing to take, and spell that out in clearly defined terms. It's a good idea to list all the "chores" that will have to be done once the pet is a part of the household, and divide them up among the family members based on which jobs each person is willing to commit to on a permanent basis. If parents discover that nobody wants to do the more onorous chores like cleaning the birdcage or the litter box, they'll have a clue about how things will go when the pet actually arrives. It's up to the parents to set limits on how responsibility should be shared.

—How much money can we afford to spend on a pet? How much per month can we allocate for food, veterinary care, boarding while we're away, and other regular expenses? Children can visit grocery stores with parents to check the prices of food various pets might need, and then talk about what it costs for licenses, annual shots, emergencies, and other ordinary expenses. This can be an opportunity for parents to teach practical lessons about planning, budgeting, and taking responsibility for our actions.

—Is the size and energy level of the pet we're considering appropriate for our family? Is it too big (or too small) for the children to handle easily? Is it safe? Could this animal harm a child? It's remarkable how many families blindly choose a "macho" dog—a Doberman or a pit bull, for example—without consideration for the safety and peace of mind of the children in the home. Children can be terrorized when they're forced to live with animals that threaten them or play too rough. Aggressive dogs usually come from a long line of "working dogs," and they don't belong with children who can't control them.

—What will happen if the pet we're considering doesn't meet our needs as well as we hope? Family members should talk about how they will deal with this possibility. Again, planning can help avoid problems.

You know the old, familiar story. Mom and Dad get a cat or dog for Junior because he promises a thousand times that he'll feed it, walk it, groom it, and take it everywhere. Mom and Dad, suckers that they are, tell themselves a pet might be a good idea because it will teach Junior to be responsible. Usually in about a month Junior begins to "forget" the feeding and walking, and soon Mom, Dad, and Junior are bickering constantly about the responsibilities Junior seems to be shirking. Saddest of all, the pet becomes a burden instead of a cherished member of the family. How can parents keep this sort of thing from happening?

It's a bad idea to get a pet to "teach responsibility." It almost always boomerangs. What actually happens is that kids learn to *resent* and *avoid* responsibility—and that's a terrible lesson that ends up hurting kids, parents, *and* pets.

This relates to the "waiting period" I talked about before. Parents have to evaluate how much responsibility each child is actually able to take for a pet based on factors like age, past experience, maturity, and a realistic appraisal of the child's motivation.

Don't get a pet that will be a burden to your children—or to you, if you end up having to take care of it. Regardless of how much whining and begging your kids do, firmly refuse to give in to their desire for a pet until you're positive they can *easily* handle the responsibility, and they have shown it through progressively more and more responsible actions in other areas of their lives. A child who has never taken responsibility for cleaning up his room or fixing a simple meal, for example, is not ready for the much larger responsibilities of pet ownership. Let him practice on progressively more and more responsible tasks before you allow him to enter into a relationship with a pet.

As parents, we have to balance what's possible and reasonable to expect from our children with the child's true motivations. During your "waiting period" you'll have the time to see what the child really wants from a pet, and you can then decide whether it's merely a passing phase or something more enduring. If your child says, "Everyone has a dog," or complains that "My friend Jennifer has a kitten, so I should have one, too," you'll know that her real motivation is simply to own something everyone else

*T*he day is young, said the cat, remembering that he could wait.

owns—like a new pair of shoes or a T-shirt. When the fad wears off, the pet will be tossed aside just the way the shoes and T-shirt are when they're no longer new and exciting. Instead of giving in, you can simply wait for the desire to pass.

Look for signs that the child is interested in a long-term *relationship* with the pet. After all, a family pet's biggest function in our lives is to fulfill our needs—both emotionally and spiritually. If it doesn't do that, it becomes nothing more than a nuisance in our lives. That's sad—both for the pet and its owners. How does your child do in relationships with friends? Do you see compassion, empathy, and the desire to anticipate and meet others' needs in your child's behavior—or do you see selfishness and a lack of interest in others? Don't expect that your child will magically transform into a compassionate, caring person if he isn't that way *before* you get a pet. Look for evidence that the child wants more than just another toy.

Another problem that seems to come up in the area of responsibility is the matter of what happens when a pet simply doesn't work out. Parents too often force the issue, demanding that their children take responsibility for the fate of the animal when they may be incapable of doing so. A good rule is that children should never be forced to be parents. And asking a young child to decide the fate of a pet is doing just that. It teaches even *more* resentment of responsibility instead of helping the child grow. Parents have to deal with reality. Before a pet is brought home, parents should decide what they'll do if their child isn't able to handle the pet—in spite of their best efforts to assure success. They should develop a contingency plan, because that's realistic. A child doesn't learn anything good when his parents simply dispose of a pet like a broken toy and then tell him it's his fault.

How can we help a child—or another adult, for that matter—deal with the death of a pet?

One of the sad facts about relationships with animals is that we can expect to lose them long before we would lose a human companion to death. Even a very long-lived dog or cat will not normally live beyond fifteen or sixteen years. Some larger dogs live much shorter lives. It may help ease the pain of a pet's death if it grows old with the family. There can be a gradual winding down of the relationship as the animal grows older; the family can take time to get used to the idea that this pet will not live much longer. They can prepare for the separation together. If you have the chance to prepare, you can begin to grieve before the fact. But when pets die in accidents or simply disappear from our lives, or when they die from heart attacks or unexpected illnesses, the grieving process is complicated by shock.

It seems to be hardest of all when we must make the decision to put a pet to sleep because it's in pain or has an irreversible disease. Children need help dealing with the sometimes over-whelming feelings of loss, guilt, sadness, and fear that are generated when we must make that choice.

It's a mistake to tell children (or adults, for that matter) not to feel sad, not to cry, or not to think about the loss of a pet. Never dismiss the death of a beloved animal by saying "it was *only* a dog (or cat, gerbil, turtle, or bird)." That attitude demeans and devalues the positive feelings and genuine love that were expe-rienced in a very real and important relationship. The loss of a pet will mean that those who loved the pet will mourn, and that mourning should be permitted and respected in the family. It isn't very different from the mourning that takes place when we lose the people we love.

The death of a pet can be an opportunity for families to talk about loss and sadness. Parents can talk about the pets they've lost in the past and how they handled their grief. The family can cry together and allow each other to grieve individually, sympa-thizing and comforting each other in special ways. People don't usually get much understanding or help from outside the family when a pet dies. If I said to someone, "My mother died," I'd get great sympathy, but if I said, "My cat died," I'd get very little. Most people would say, "Too bad," and let it go at that. But the depth of our grief over the loss of a pet can be just as significant as in the loss of a member of the family, depending on the closeness of the human or animal relationship. We need to experience that grief, not stifle it.

Sometimes it helps a family to have a funeral for a pet. It's a means of saying final farewells. It acknowledges that death has taken place and the relationship is over. In my own childhood we had an elaborate funeral when our dog died. We sang hymns, gathered flowers, and made a wreath for the service we held at the grave, which was in a field near the house. Over the years that followed, we visited the grave with fresh flowers and remembered the good years we had together. Some friends of ours had a pet cemetery for all the pets that died in their family. I thought it was a good idea—it gave appropriate dignity and importance to the animals that had enriched their lives.

Another thing that can be helpful is simply to reminisce about the pet and the things that were unique about it. As a family you can visit the places your pet played, look at photographs, and even put mementoes like a collar, a food dish, or a favorite toy in a special place of honor. All of this will enable the family to further the process of grieving which will finally allow everyone to move forward.

The mourning process with pets can last anywhere from a few days to many months, just as it can with people. It's quite individual. I remember a little boy I counseled whose cat died. He cried and grieved over the loss of the cat far more deeply than he did over the really enormous problems he was facing in his family. Actually, the rule about grieving is that it's different for everyone, and we have to allow for those differences and let people do what they must to get through it.

Parents naturally worry if children seem to be carrying their sadness too long, but I think they should be more concerned when their children don't seem to grieve at all. Occasionally grief can become exaggerated and unhealthy, and that's usually pretty obvious—the loss crowds out everything else in life for many months or perhaps years. In those rare cases professional counseling might be helpful. But most of the time the healthiest thing is for the grieving person to work through the pain with the support of those who understand and permit the process to be thoroughly accomplished. That's what family members should be able to do.

Gradually, depending on the length and intensity of the relationship between people and pet, recovery begins. Thoughts about the animal become less frequent, and we begin to shift from thoughts of death toward thoughts of life. We find that we can talk about the pet and it hurts less than it did a month ago. We're able to remember the good times without crying. There may be moments when grief unexpectedly wells up again, and that may go on for years, but eventually—in our own time—we heal.

Is it a good idea to try to bring a new pet into the family as soon as possible to help ease the feelings of loss?

Not always, but it really depends on the family. Some need to wait until the pain of the loss has completely healed. Others may not need extended periods of mourning. As important as grief can be, it's just as important not to force anyone to grieve, or to make him feel guilty for not being sad for a long time. Sometimes a child will begin to recover from a loss by *asking* for a new pet. In those cases, there's nothing wrong with talking it over as a family and deciding it's time for another animal. But remember, we can never truly *replace* any pet. Each one has a unique spot in our hearts, and it's unfair to expect a new animal to take the place of one that dies.

Hoping to distract a child from his grief, many parents quickly bring in a new pet they expect to erase all the painful memories of the one that's died. Unfortunately, this doesn't usually spare the child any pain. What it really does is deny him the privilege of mourning. It's often wisest to take a few months out for grieving the loss of one pet before bringing another on the scene. Rushing into a new dog or cat may suggest to a child that those we love are easily disposed of and replaced. Sometimes a child will have secret fears that because his parents seemed to feel no pain over the loss of a pet and quickly "replaced" it with another, they might be capable of doing the same thing with him. Children need to be reassured that the people and animals they love are irreplaceable and are never forgotten. They also need to learn from experience that the pain of loss eventually gets better, and we go on with life. It's through such experiences that children can gain the courage to open themselves to loving relationships with new animals (and people) in spite of the fact that they may one day part.

My husband and I had a golden retriever named Taffy who was stolen when she was a year and a half old. I had grown terribly attached to her, and it was very hard for me to get over that loss. I was so upset, in fact, that I made up my mind never to get attached to an animal again. But eventually I finished grieving and realized that the process had stretched me as a person. I made a decision not to remain detached, not to ignore and shut out the animals that could be a wonderful, joyous part of my life. I wanted the fun and pleasure that animals could bring, so eventually I chose to take the risk that comes with attachment. That's an important step for all of us. With animals as with people, love carries with it the possibility of loss and pain. But if we don't accept that possibility, we miss a lot of love and our lives are poorer for it.

How do you answer children when they ask if their pet has gone to heaven?

I avoid dogmatic responses. Parents often mistake a child's questions about where the dead animal has gone as a request for theological answers. That's almost never the case. Kids don't think in those terms. Actually, they're looking for two distinct things: First, to have their emotions satisfied, and second, to get a clear, satisfying visual picture of where the pet is now.

Children often have scary, unsettling fears about death which lead them to picture their pets (and people, too) trapped under the cold, damp earth without anyone to take care of them. Parents can help children satisfy the emotional need for reassurance by explaining that the pet is not "down there"—that it has left behind its skin and bones and has gone to a place where it's safe and warm, where it can be taken care of and loved just as well as it was by the child.

To help a child get the visual picture that will comfort him best, parents can ask the child, "What kind of place do you think God would create for the pet you and He love so much?" Allow the child to fantasize about the perfect eternal home for the pet. Parents are often delighted and surprised by the elaborate, colorful fantasies their children have about what heaven should be like for a pet. If a child says, "I think Tinkerbell is somewhere

in outer space playing in a big glass house full of catnip and Meow Mix," a parent can say, "I'd like to think that, too. That sounds like just the kind of thing God might have in store for her." This sort of discussion can be enormously comforting, both for the child and for the parent. When the parent avoids getting caught up in theological answers the child can't comprehend anyway, a real opportunity for communication occurs. And the child begins to understand God in terms he or she *can* relate to—visual pictures representing safety, love, comfort and joy.

Through this whole process, parents will find many chances to insure that kids learn positive lessons about relationships, loss, God, and love. Above all, when families face the loss of a treasured animal, they need to reassure each other that God loves animals *and* people, and that He will provide whatever is best and most perfect for each of us.

Pet Prints

Award-winning artist Pat McLaughlin, whose charming drawings of cats appear in this book, makes her work available to the public in the form of signed and numbered limited-edition prints and on note cards and stationery. Most of her depictions of pets are taken from real-life animals whose owners supply her with photos. Owners whose pets become McLaughlin originals are given the first signed print in the series. Write for her catalog: Art Studio Workshops, 518 Schilling Circle, N.W., Forest Lake, Minnesota 55025; (612) 464-5623.

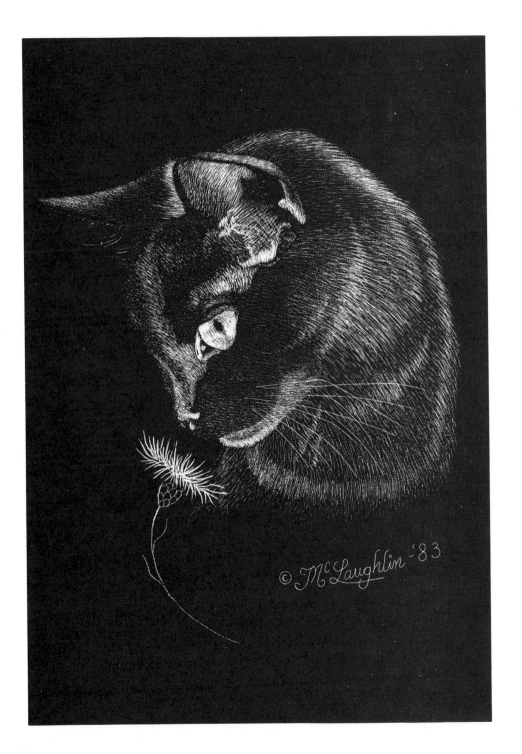

© McLaughlin '83

Pets for People

Thousands of senior citizens around the country are now being matched with dogs and cats through a new pet adoption program offered by Ralston Purina Company and local humane societies and SPCAs. The Pets for People Program unites people sixty years of age or older with homeless shelter pets completely free of charge.

More than ninety animal shelters in seventy cities are offering the program. Purina donates $100 to the shelter for each pet adopted by a senior citizen. The donation covers the adoption fee and a complete health checkup by a veterinarian (including inoculations and spaying and neutering) for each pet. Prospective pet owners are carefully screened to be sure the animals will get plenty of love and affection and that their practical needs will be met. Each newly adopted pet comes with a free starter supply of dog or cat food, a new leash, food and water bowls, and a booklet on how to take care of the pet. In return, owners attend an orientation session to learn the responsibilities of caring for a pet and agree to give the pet a good home. Later, the program staff checks with owners to be sure they're getting along well and that the animals are in good hands.

Most program participants choose cats and dogs that are at least a year old. Adult pets are ideal for older people because they're usually trained and housebroken. Their manners are generally better than those of puppies and kittens, and they don't need as much care.

The matches that have been made in the first year of the program have proven beneficial to both the pets and their new owners. Many owners have discovered that their new furry friends are better for their health than any tonic or medicine they've tried. A number of studies have shown that pets can be instrumental in speeding recovery from illness, lowering blood pressure, and curing depression—a common problem among older people. Pets reduce feelings of isolation and loneliness that can plague those who retire from an active life or are suddenly living alone after many years of marriage. Pets even increase their owners' resistance to disease by providing a source of love, comfort, and security. Research has shown that the quality of life can dramatically improve when an older person has a pet to look after.

Participants in the Pets for People Program agree. A survey of those who first adopted pets showed that nearly 100 percent said their pet was a good friend or companion, 97 percent felt happier since they had gotten the pet, and 93 percent felt less lonely. And the vast majority said they felt healthier and that their pet gave them an added incentive to exercise.

With more than 8 million elderly Americans living alone and many more millions of unwanted animals in animal shelters, the time seems right for these two groups to get together in a mutually rewarding way.

For applications or information, call your local shelter or write the Purina Pets for People Program, Checkerboard Square, St. Louis, Missouri 63164.

The Ten Commandments of Pet Ownership

by Dr. Michael W. Fox

Pets give people lots of pleasure. In return, people should treat pets right. If you're a pet owner, commit yourself to these 10 basic rules:

1. *Treat all companion animals humanely—with patience, compassion, understanding, and consideration for their needs.*

Humane treatment is what we owe pets in return for their wonderful companionship and unconditional affection. Being humane to all creatures also helps us become better people.

2. *Promise to uphold your pet's basic rights.*

Bringing a new animal home is like taking in a new child. Before you decide to have a pet, be sure you can give it the time, attention, and proper care it's entitled to.

All animals have the right to a clean and quiet place to sleep. No pets should be allowed to roam free and unsupervised.

3. *Give your pets fresh water and a complete and balanced diet daily.*

Clean your pet's water bowl and fill with fresh water every day. Likewise, always give it a variety of food that's fresh, not stale. Buy foods that offer a complete and balanced diet.

4. *Know the needs of your pet and fulfill them as best as you possibly can.*

Read about the type of pet you have and about its particular needs. Most animals require regular exercise, playtime, companionship, and grooming. Most also enjoy the company of their own kind.

5. *Give your pet regular veterinary care.*

All pets are likely to get sick at some time. You should be prepared to pay for veterinary treatment. Read up on the signs of illness your pet can show. These can include disinterest in food or water and being less playful and less responsive to you. Frequent sneezing, difficult breathing, a discharge from the nose or eyes, diarrhea, and displays of aggressive behavior when touched signal that your pet needs to go to the animal doctor.

6. *It's wrong for people to take an animal from the wild and keep it for a pet.*

Wild animals belong in the wild, not in captivity. Keeping a raccoon or fox in a small cage, for example, is cruel and inhumane.

Raising an orphaned baby rabbit or bird until it's old enough to be released back into the wild is fine. But resist the temptation to try to make such wildlife into pets.

7. *Watch your animal and learn to understand its behavior.*

Being very attentive and interpreting your animal's behavior carefully will help you avoid punishing it unfairly. Some examples: it's natural for puppies to chew things up, because they are teething. Cats and dogs sometimes become unhousebroken because of an infection or because they are upset by the presence of a new pet or baby in the home. Animals often bite when they are afraid or in pain. Don't punish pets for any of these behaviors. If necessary, take them to a vet, who can determine what the problem is.

8. *Give your pet obedience training.*

Your dog should be trained so it won't bother other people and so it will be easy to handle. Always keep your dog on a leash outdoors and train it to obey such simple commands as "sit," "stay," and "come." And *never* strike an animal. A firm and sharp command is enough.

9. *When euthanasia is required, make sure the animal dies painlessly and with dignity.*

"Euthanasia" means humane death. Ten to 13 million unwanted cats and dogs are euthanized in animal shelters each year—because irresponsible owners fail to have their pets neutered to prevent breeding.

But there are times when euthanasia is the best choice: when an animal is so old, sick or injured that its health cannot be restored. It's far better to end, rather than prolong, incurable suffering.

10. *Everyone who cares about animals should defend any animal being treated inhumanely. And they should share with others these 10 Commandments of Pet Ownership.*

Whenever you see someone mistreating an animal, immediately report it to your local animal control authority or the police. Animals are our companions, so we should be their protectors. I call this *humane stewardship.* For all the many ways they enrich our lives, it's the least we can do.

Pet Population

There are an estimated 58 million cats living in American homes. Also, 52 million dogs, 45 million birds, 260 million fish (give or take a guppy), and another 125 million other creatures are kept as pets.

Want to Help Animals?

The *Animal Activist's Handbook*, available from the Animal Protection Institute (P.O. Box 22505, Sacramento, California 95822) will tell you everything you need to know to get started. This comprehensive, beautifully illustrated guide (complete with numerous case histories) tells you how to go about making the world a safer, sounder place for animals regardless of where you live. 103 pages, $2.75.

Also available from the Institute:

- Bookmarks: "Purr-fect Care of Cats" (Dog and bird bookmarks also available). Lists responsibilities of animal ownership. Great for kids. 100 for $2.00.
- Colorful stamps featuring art from API's children's art contests.
- Bumper stickers: "Stand Up For Animals"; "Be An Animal's Best Friend." $1.00.
- Window decal for house or car: "Animals Inside." 50¢ each.
- T-Shirts: "Stand Up For Animals." S-M-L, Children's size, $8.00. Adult S-M-L-XL, $10.00 (for men or women).
- "Finding Good Homes for Pets." Free brochure.
- "How to Become Involved For Animals in Your Community." Free brochure.
- Children's Reading List. 35¢.
- Cat Care, Dog Care brochures. 15¢.
- Posters: Large, beautiful, and colorful—a natural for kids' rooms and offices.

The Pettable Kingdom Mystery Poster	$2.00
How to Care for Your Pet	$2.00
Wildlife Under Attack	$3.00

- Sun shields for cars: Accordion-fold heavy-duty shields to place inside your front window. One side asks for help in an emergency; the other says, "Don't Park Your Pet" and explains the problems of heat stroke when animals are left inside cars on warm days.

How Children See Their Pets

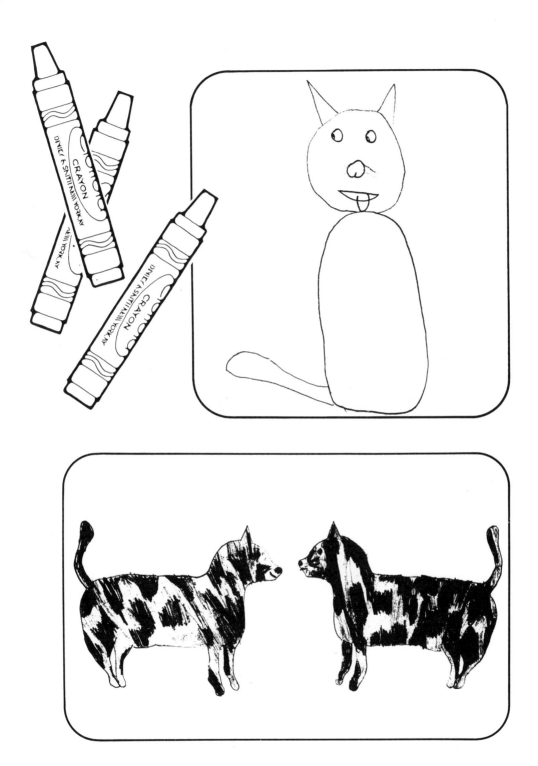

Test Your Pet I.Q.

by Francis Sheridan Goulart

A well-informed pet owner provides the best TLC for his cat or dog. How much of what you know about your cat or dog is on target? Test it out. The following information is provided by the Pets Are Wonderful Council (PAW), the American Kennel Society, the American Humane Society, and the American Feline Society.

True or False?

1. No one has ever died from a dog bite.
   Answer: False. Dogs put the bite on one million of us a year, the *American Medical Journal* says, and although it's rare, a dog's bite *can* be fatal.
2. Cat lovers spend $2 billion a year on cat food.
   Answer: True.
3. The average dog is as smart as a three- to four-year-old child.
   Answer: True.
4. Hamburger is a good food for adult dogs.
   Answer: False—too much fat.
5. It costs $300 to take care of a medium-size dog for one year.
   Answer: False. It's closer to $400, the Humane Society says.
6. A neutered cat gets fat, and there's nothing you can do.
   Answer: False. Neutering changes the metabolism, but exercise and proper feeding will prevent obesity.
7. The gentlest of the big dogs and the one least likely to bite is the Labrador retriever.
   Answer: True.
8. A high-fish diet every day is not good for cats.
   Answer: True. It can cause yellow fat disease.
9. You can't teach an old dog new tricks.
   Answer: False. Older dogs actually learn faster.
10. Every U.S. president has owned a cat or a dog.

Answer: False. The six presidents who never owned anything feathered or furry were John Adams, James K. Polk, Millard Fillmore, Franklin Pierce, James Buchanan, and Chester Arthur, the Dog Museum of America says.

11. Chocolate and milk give puppies worms.

Answer: False. Milk is fine, but chocolate can make a puppy sick.

12. You can catch a cold from your cat.

Answer: False. But cats can transmit streptococcus bacilli, as well as lice, rabies, and pinworms.

13. Dogs obey men better than they obey women.

Answer: True. Dogs respond to a deeper tone of voice, but when a woman has an authoritative tone, a dog does just as well.

14. The dog name "Fido" means "faithful."

Answer: True.

15. The most popular name for the bulldog in the U.S. is Spot.

Answer: False. It's Winston.

16. Pets should be kept warmer than people.

Answer: False. An overly warm house can disturb a cat or dog's thermostat and cause hypothermia.

17. A small dog is easier to train than a large one.

Answer: False. Size is not a major factor in training a dog.

18. Canine distemper is no longer a problem in the U.S.

Answer: False. There are still enough cases to warrant vaccinations.

19. Cats never need people.

Answer: False. They can become just as attached to their owners as can dogs.

20. Dogs see everything in black and white.

Answer: True.

21. Unspayed female dogs often die of cancer.

Answer: True.

22. Dogs and cats are natural enemies.

Answer: False. Dogs and cats can live together harmoniously.

23. Purebreds are smarter than mixed breeds.

Answer: False. There is no difference.

24. There are more pet dogs than cats in the U.S.

Answer: False. For the first time, cats are in the majority.

25. The four most popular "color" names for dogs are Blackie, Midnight, Yellow, and Rusty.

Answer: True.

26. When a cat rubs against you he's expressing affection.

Answer: False. He's making you a part of his territory by rubbing his scent on you.

27. Shaving a dog's coat in summer will keep him cool.

Answer: False. A dog's coat insulates him against both heat and cold. The coat protects him from sunburn and insects, including mosquitoes, which can carry heart-worms.

28. The normal dog needs only one or two baths a year.

Answer: True. Frequent baths wash vitamins and natural oils from the coat.

29. Cats came to America with the Pilgrims in the 1600s.

Answer: True.

30. Dogs don't like living in apartments.

Answer: False. Dogs are happy as long as they get food, discipline, exercise, and TLC.

31. A dog or puppy best loves the person who feeds him.

Answer: True.

32. Feline Leukemia, a cancer in cats, can now be prevented by vaccination.

Answer: True.

33. All pets need lots of exercise.

Answer: False. Only dogs bred for hunting and herding have high exercise requirements. And cats thrive on moderate activity.

34. A dog should be trained by only one member of the family.

Answer: False. Every member of the family should help.

35. Cats are the only clawed animals that walk on their paws, not their claws.

Answer: True.

36. The Pekingese was regarded as sacred by Oriental royalty.

Answer: True.

37. Once a dog has had guard-dog training, he can't be untrained.

Answer: True.

38. Cats don't have a sweet tooth, but dogs do.

Answer: True.

Hamlet: The Tail Is Told

The historic Algonquin Hotel in the middle of New York City's theater district has long served as a luxurious home-away-from-home for actors, writers, and other celebrities. Today the Algonquin is also the home of a tabby cat that was rescued, half-starved and at death's door, by the North Shore Animal League of Port Washington, New York. The Algonquin's director, Andrew Anspach, arranged for the hotel to make the cat a part of its family through the League's adoption center, where thousands of animals each year are rescued from euthanasia and then are fed and housed while they await new homes. The Algonquin cat was taken in when he was only eight months old. His days as a stray are only a dim memory; now he lives the life of royalty. "I guess we spoil him," Anspach says. "But it's obvious he's a real prince. He even wears a silver bell which says—'Hamlet of the Algonquin.' "

Cat Heroes

Animals are the best kind of heroes. They're selfless, they act without concern for their own welfare, and they never brag. If modesty is the better part of heroism, then animals are heroes of the first magnitude. Surely they deserve more than the medals and silver bowls they receive each year via the hero award programs that recognize their acts. At the very least, they deserve our admiration and respect—and we'd be hard-pressed to deny that any one of our animal heroes deserves a pat on the head from its Master and a heartfelt "Well done, thou good and faithful servant."

Matterhorn Cat, a four-month-old black-and-white stray kitten, climbed the Matterhorn in Switzerland in 1950. The kitten apparently had been born somewhere on the premises of the Hotel Belvedere on the ridge where mountain climbers usually began their ascents of the 14,780-foot peak. After watching a group of climbers begin their trek up the mountain one August morning, the kitten decided to follow. He was soon left behind, and the climbers didn't see him again until they bedded down in a hut at the 12,556-foot level. The cat, a bit disheveled but otherwise in good shape, arrived before nightfall and spent the night with the climbers.

The next day the cat kept pace with the climbing party, scaling the mountain with apparent ease. He slept among the rocks some distance from his human competitors. The next morning he was noticed by the climbers as they passed him headed for the extremely difficult phase of the climb known as the Ropes, the Slabs, and the Roof. The climbers assumed the kitten could not proceed further, since it would be impossible for him to cross the large chasms that lay ahead.

They were mistaken. When the party reached the summit of the Matterhorn the kitten greeted them enthusiastically. They rewarded and congratulated him with a share of their dinner.

The guide who led the climbing group, not wanting to leave the kitten on the summit, carried him in his backpack down to the 12,700-foot level, leaving him for a party returning to the hotel to take him home. The kitten had other plans. He decided to remain at the higher elevation and was seen for some years after that by climbing parties, who enjoyed watching the happy, well-fed cat hunt for mice. There were no reports that he ever climbed to the summit again, however.

Oscar, the pet Siamese cat of the J. R. Williams family of Conroe, Texas, was named a Friskies Hero Cat in the 1970s for doing what comes naturally for Siamese cats: Oscar howled.

Oscar is normally as quiet as a cat can be, so when his young neighbors, Robin Smith, thirteen, and Weaver Wiggins, eight, heard him howling and scratching at the window of his house, they felt sure Oscar was trying to tell them something. The something, it turned out, was a fire in the kitchen of the Williams home. The boys ran for help, the fire was extinguished, and Oscar came out of it with his Hero award—and some fringe benefits. The annual Friskies Hero Cat Award, promoted by the Carnation Company, brings with it an engraved silver feeding bowl, a $100 savings bond, and a year's supply of cat food.

Melissa, a three-year-old white cat from Denver, won the Friskies Hero Cat Award by distracting a knife-wielding robber long

enough for her mistress to run out of her Denver bookstore and call the police. Melissa's twenty-six-year-old mistress had been accosted and threatened by the robber, who at knife-point demanded all the the money from her cash register. Melissa sprang at the intruder, attacking and hissing at him fiercely. The robber, fighting off the attack, finally grabbed a chair to strike the cat, and while he was distracted, Melissa's mistress ran next door for help. The thief fled. Police credited the cat with averting the robbery and possibly saving her mistress's life. Melissa modestly refused to comment on the affair.

Punky, a thirteen-year-old cat of undetermined breed but indisputable courage, waited twelve long years for fame, fortune, and a Hero Cat award. In 1965 Punky saved the life of her then two-year-old infant mistress in Riverdale, Maryland. The baby was endangered by a poisonous copperhead snake which Punky fearlessly attacked and killed. It was not until 1977, when Punky's mistress grew up, that she nominated her pet for the award.

Sam, a cross-eyed Manx, received double distinction for his heroic efforts in saving his family from their blazing home. In addition to receiving the Hero Cat Award for 1974, Sam was

made an honorary fireman by the Orange, California, fire station that responded to the fire.

Py, an eight-year-old gray tabby from Williamsburg, Virginia, used step-by-step reasoning powers to protect her mistress from a prowler. When Py spotted a suspicious man in the garden of Elsie George's small home in the Colonial Williamsburg Restoration area, she took five thoughtful steps: 1. She awakened her mistress by jumping on her stomach; 2. she reawakened her, jumping on her back; 3. she led her downstairs to the front door; 4. she then ignored Miss George's suggestion that she go outside; and finally, 5. she streaked back upstairs and sat on a dark windowsill, peering pointedly at the moving shadow.

Miss George finally got the message and called the police. They apprehended the suspect, who had already slit the screen door to enter the house. Py became the Friskies Hero Cat of 1973 for her efforts.

Rhubarb was a part-Siamese cat who spent seventeen years as a seeing-eye companion for her blind mistress, Mrs. Elsie Schneider, of San Diego, California. Rhubarb did everything for her mistress that a seeing-eye dog would.

Mrs. Schneider, who was blinded ten years before Rhubarb came into her life, trained the cat while she was still a kitten. After sitting through training sessions for dogs at a sightless people's club, Mrs. Schneider decided to try to train her kitten to respond to all the signals and commands that would make her into a true seeing-eye cat. Rhubarb proved to be an apt pupil, and the two of them lived independently in a normal house all the years they were together. In the morning, the cat always led Mrs. Schneider through her

regular chores, including laundry, gardening, and household cleaning. Wearing a special harness, the cat took her mistress to shops and grocery stores, protecting Mrs. Schneider from stray animals and handling traffic just as a seeing-eye dog would. The cat always considered Mrs. Schneider her sole occupation.

When Rhubarb died on April 4, 1980, she was nominated for the only Hero Cat of the Decade Award ever given by the Friskies Cat Council. Her mistress accepted the award on behalf of Rhubarb at a special ceremony at San Diego's Pet Memorial Park on National Pet Memorial Day that same year.

The Legend of the Pussy Willow

Once, many years ago, an unkind farmer pitched a litter of soft gray kittens into the river to drown. Much distraught, the mama cat paced the riverbank, weeping so loudly and so long that the willows nearby took pity on her: they dipped their long branches into the cold, rushing water, and the kittens took hold, clung dearly, and were saved. For their great act of kindness, Spring declared that the soft velvet buds of the pussy willow would evermore be the first sign of her entrance—the rebirth of Spring.

—Polish Folk Tale

A Best Friend for Kevin

by Catherine Vanicek

Kevin was the kind of boy all the other kids made fun of. No matter how spruced and polished he appeared when he left for school in the morning, he was sure to come home a mess. No matter how hard he strained to decipher the words that all the other kids could read with ease, the letters still insisted on shifting around on the page, scrambling themselves into the disjointed circles and sticks which were as foreign to him as hieroglyphics or Chinese. Dyslexic the teachers called him; stupid his schoolmates tagged him, a failure he was forced to feel.

"Mrs. Ryan you've got to find something to raise Kevin's self-esteem," Constance Brimstead, Kevin's special education counselor, informed the boy's mother the morning Kevin threw little Lucy Carter's crayons across the room at the giant mural covering the far wall. "He has absolutely no confidence in himself, and it's beginning to affect him psychologically."

Dismayed, Colleen Ryan swept a stray wisp of blonde hair back off of her face and met the other woman's steady, gray gaze. Being a working mother was no breeze; being a single, working mother was even more of a challenge. Still, she was positive she'd been coping.

"Affect his psyche. How so?"

"Well, you can see for yourself that he's disturbed. For over a week now the students have been taking turns working on this mural for open house. Angela Jennings drew that simply marvelous tree in the left-hand corner there, Jesse Martinez sketched in that beautiful rainbow over Amy Wilkins's mountains, and Gini Chang bordered the side of Jimmy Cousin's little yellow house with a bed of colorful flowers. But your son Kevin. . . . Well, just look!" And so saying she made a sweeping gesture toward a large, dark blob sitting defiantly atop Sandi Grover's immaculate white picket fence.

Colleen took in her son's contribution to the class project with an amused sigh. Not even a mother's loving eye could find much to praise there.

"He's certainly no artist," she agreed wryly.

Assuming her most professional demeanor, the other woman reached out to tap the offending blob with the tip of her finger. The nail was ragged and bitten to the quick.

"Really, Mrs. Ryan I don't think you understand the seriousness of what I'm saying here. Kevin's talent or lack of talent is *not* the issue. His mental state is. It is not normal for an eight-year-old boy to draw a frightening black monster with a blood red gash on it right in the middle of such a sunny, tranquil scene!"

"Monster? *What* monster?" Kevin demanded, after being readmitted to the room while the other students were at P.E.

Mrs. Brimstead's patience was growing thin. Once more her finger stabbed the convoluted blob.

"There, on the fence. The black and red monster you drew."

Kevin's face darkened indignantly. His blue eyes took on the look of storm-tossed seas. "That's no monster! That's Jasper, my cat."

A pause then, *"Cat?"*

"Yes, cat. Tell her, Mom. Make her take it back! Jasper's no monster. He's the best cat in the whole world. He's the best cat there ever was!"

Colleen turned from her son to the school counselor, her normally pleasant face a carefully studied blank. She didn't know whether to laugh aloud in relief or to fume at the injustice. She certainly couldn't cry.

A look of chagrin crept over Mrs. Brimstead's face, but she had to understand. "Why does your cat have that red streak cutting across it? Is it hurt?"

"Nah, of course not. That's his collar. It's red."

The older woman's face suffused with color. Slowly she turned to the child's mother for confirmation. Things were certainly not going at all as she had expected.

"Jasper's collar *is* red," Colleen contributed. Indignation was fighting to make itself felt, but her son's vindication should come from his own lips.

"In fact," she added, "Kevin chose it himself shortly after he picked Jasper out at the S.P.C.A. He said the collar made him look special; made him look like someone cared about him a lot." Then laying her arm across her son's shoulders and drawing him close for an affectionate hug, she prompted, "Why don't you tell Mrs. Brimstead about Jasper, honey?"

Kevin had not forgotten the slur on his work. But Jasper was important to the third grader, and he could not resist rushing into speech.

"I got Jasper last year for my report card. I was lonely a lot 'cause kids make fun of me and all. You know what I mean? So then I told Mom I really needed a good friend, and she said if I worked real, real hard and Teacher said I did as good as I could, I could have any cat I wanted for a prize.

"So Mom brought me home some cat-care books to practice my reading on, and I studied my "b's" and my "d's," and by the end of the year they didn't switch 'round on me any more—well, almost they didn't. And even though my reading grade still wasn't so good, Teacher did say I tried hard, so I got Jasper for my very own. Which was a good thing, too. You know why?"

Mrs. Brimstead couldn't resist smiling at the boy's earnest expression. His hair stuck up every which way and the end of one pant-leg was caught up in his sock, but she had never seen him so sincere.

"No I don't, Kevin. Why?"

" 'Cause even though the S.P.C.A. saves animals from mean people who hurt them and everything, they don't get no love there. I know 'cause when I saw Jasper in his cage his coat was full of all kinds of knots and he was skinny and ascared and crying and he wanted to go home with me real, real bad. And if I hadn't worked on my letters so hard, Jasper wouldn't never have had a home or love which is sad 'cause he's a real great cat."

A sudden burst of understanding stung Mrs. Brimstead's eyes

and tightened painfully in her throat. Kevin wasn't exaggerating about not having many friends. Other children didn't relate well to those who were different from themselves, and Kevin was different. Yet different, she now suspected, in a sweet special way.

She blinked twice, then cleared a lump from her throat. The boy had heart.

"Not only is Jasper a 'real great cat,' " she said earnestly, "but he's a lucky one, too. To belong to a nice boy like you, I mean."

"Oh, yes," Kevin agreed solemnly. "And did you know that I brush him every day so that he doesn't get hairballs in his stomach and throw up all over the rug?"

Taken aback, the counselor vouchsafed that she didn't.

"Well, it's true. And I also keep his water bowl and his food dish clean, and I change his litter box. It's 'portant if I want him to stay healthy, you know. And I want Jasper to stay healthy 'cause he's my friend. My best friend. That's why I drew him on the mural. He never thinks I'm stupid like the other kids do."

Kneeling down on a level to match his own, Colleen Ryan asked gently, "Has someone recently called you stupid, son?"

Kevin's young face took on the look she had witnessed there so many times before. The look that was a mixture of hurt and of anger, of disappointment and of trampled pride.

"Lucy Carter," he mumbled. "She said my drawing of Jasper was ugly. She said I'm stupid 'cause I can't read. But when the letters hold still I *can* read. I can. Besides, Jasper's not ugly; I took care of him, and he grew into a great cat."

There was pride in that statement, and Colleen Ryan decided it was time to take matters in hand.

The morning after open house, Kevin catapulted into room 11-B. He was excited, and when Kevin was excited there was no holding him down.

"Children," Mrs. Brimstead announced as Colleen helped her son withdraw a startled, amber-eyed, black-coated form from the well-ventilated animal carrier placed on the teacher's desk before him, "today we have a very special surprise for you. Today Kevin Ryan is going to tell you all about the proper way to take care of a cat.

"It's an important subject, I'm sure you'll agree, and one about which Kevin is particularly . . ." she paused to search for a word, ". . . and one about which Kevin is particularly . . . smart.

"I want you to be nice and quiet now, because we don't want to frighten Jasper with too much noise. But once Kevin is through teaching you, I'm sure he'll be happy to answer your questions. Kevin,"—this as the room buzzed with anticipation—"we're ready for you."

Colleen stepped back and away. The idea had been hers, but Kevin was very knowledgeable about his favorite topic and he deserved center stage. She had no illusions about what they were accomplishing—not really. For a while her son would be the focus of attention; the hero of the hour; the schoolmate who had changed a dreary work-a-day morning into one of eagerness and fun. But inevitably the tomorrows would come and a lot of the children would go back to their old patterns.

Still, if one or two continued to see in Kevin what Mrs.

Brimstead now saw; if Jasper's plump, golden-eyed presence and Kevin's carefully rehearsed speech taught even a single lonely youngster about the wealth of companionship, faith, and hope that was to be found in the ownership of the stray cats of the world, there was hope.

Besides, if all else failed—But he would not fail! Not in the long run, anyway. Not with Jasper by his side to ease his burdens with a soothing purr, to add warmth and love to his life by the simple fact of his companionable presence. No, in the long run Kevin could only prosper from the relationship.

As the boy stepped forward his mother relaxed.

"This is my friend, Jasper," Kevin began with the confidence of a young man who knows his subject front and back. "And I'm going to show you the best way to take care of a cat."

How come cats don't have to go to obedience classes?

"Ah, me—so much to do and so little time."

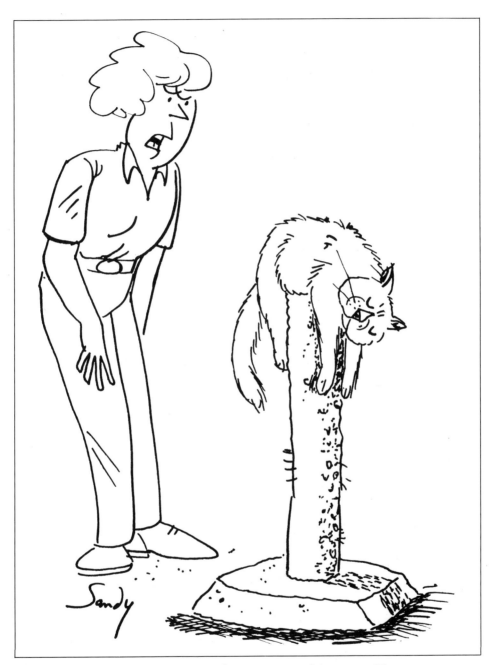

"No, No, No! *That's* a scratching *post!*"

The Cat's Page in History

by Beth Brown

The cat has played an important role in the history of civilization.

It was in ancient Egypt where the cat was first domesticated. The earliest known breed was the Caffre, or Kaffir, which is found in Egypt today. The Caffre had tabby markings and pointed ears.

Cats Revered

The early Egyptian cat led a charmed life. At the time (3500 B.C.) Egypt was the grain capital of the world, and the cat served as the custodian of her great granaries. The Egyptians treated the animal with the highest regard and the deepest reverence.

Eventually the cat was deified as the goddess Bast (also known as Ubasti and Bubastis). Bast, the goddess of moonlight, was worshiped along with the great sun god, Ra.

When a cat died, Egyptian law required members of the entire family to shave their eyebrows as a sign of mourning. Bast, goddess of life, maternity, happiness, and delight, was swathed in fine linens, embalmed, buried in mummy cases of bronze or wood, often lined with gold, and placed in a revered temple.

Egyptian tombs that have been opened in recent years have revealed not only the bodies of thousands of mummified felines, but also the bodies of tens of thousands of mummified mice, which were meant to serve as fare on the heavenly journey.

Egypt abounded with cats. They lived both with the poor in the country and in pampered luxury in the palaces of the rich. Of all the holidays celebrated through the year, the festival in honor of Bast was the most splendid. Thousands of citizens attended, traveling great distances to worship at the temple dedicated to the cat and carrying with them the mummies of their own family cats to bury in hallowed ground.

Egyptian soldiers were sent abroad to capture all the cats in sight and bring them home to Egypt. Killing a cat was a crime punishable by death.

Diodorus of Sicily reported that a Roman who had accidentally killed an Egyptian cat was attacked and torn to pieces by an angry mob.

Egypt made every effort to keep her cats within her own borders, passing a law making it illegal to export the animal. However, visiting traders often managed to smuggle them aboard their ships and sail across the Mediterranean to Europe. Here a ready market was found for the animals, both as ratters and as objects of curiosity.

Egypt's claim to being first to domesticate the cat has been challenged by some historians who say that the animal may have first been domesticated in Nubia, India, and China.

Palladius of Egypt, living in the fourth century, was the first to give the domestic cat the name of *Catus*. For many years, the tame cat in Nubia had been commonly referred to as *kadio*. Egypt had christened the male cat *kut*; the female was known as *kutta*. In Turkey the cat was called *kedi*. Cat and kitty are derived from these.

Little is known of the origin of long-haired cats such as are found in China, Angora, Burma, Russia, and Afghanistan. For a number of years, it has been claimed that the Persian emigrated from Afghanistan, its main ancestor being the Tibetan cat of Central Asia. Long-haired cats were also brought from China to Siberia, as well as into India. Cats reached Persia in the fifth or sixth century A.D. By the year A.D. 1000 they had traveled to Japan where they were valued very highly.

It is contended that a Roman soldier was the first to introduce the animal to Great Britain. Soon Scotland discovered the cat. County Caithness, meaning county of cats, was named in its honor. The Scottish goblin was represented as a cat rather than the usual figure of the nimble imp.

In Wales, cats were not only highly regarded, but protected against cruelty. In A.D. 936 Wales passed a law against cruelty to cats. The value of a kitten was computed as one penny when blind, two pennies when its eyes were open, and four pennies once it had caught a mouse.

An old Welsh law states: "If anyone steals or kills the cat which guards the prince's granary, he is to forfeit a milk ewe, its fleece and lamb, or as much wheat as when poured on the cat suspended by its tail, the head touching the floor, would form a heap high enough to cover the tip of the tail."

Cats Tortured

Not always was the cat held in such high regard, however. Because of the cat's association with pagan rites in ancient history, it was a prime suspect during the witch hunts of the Dark Ages. It was accused of employing black magic, and soon cats were persecuted.

The cat shared the fate of so-called witches, facing torture and death. During the Middle Ages, it is estimated that more than 150,000 people were charged with witchcraft in Germany and another 100,000 in France. Humans and cats were burned together. The French celebrated saints' days by collecting baskets, barrels, and sacks of cats, and tossing them upon the great fires built for the purpose in the open squares of the city.

In Picardy, on the first Sunday in Lent, the townspeople expected to be blessed by Saint John if they collected all the available cats and paraded through the streets bearing lighted torches. Then followed the ceremony of committing thousands of terrified animals to roaring flames, while the bands played merry music.

The horrible practice continued until 1604 when Louis, shocked by the sight of such torture during a festival, prevailed upon his father, King Henry IV, to issue a decree banning the rites.

The Flemish people had their own ideas of cat-torture. There they carried the cats to the tops of steeples and flung them from the heights. It wasn't until 1618 that a law was passed prohibiting the practice.

Later the cat was once again received into the household as a valued pet. Openings were made in doors and windows so that the animals could enter or leave independently. The French bred for beauty, size, and coat, and they began to pass regulations protecting the cat.

There is no record of when cats first came to be shown in public. Cats appeared at fairs and were awarded prizes for being ratters and mousers. In 1598, at the St. Giles Fair in Winchester, England, cats were shown for beauty and displayed for breed.

Cats Contribute to Civilization

Agriculture has been aided by the cat. Food has been protected. Property has been saved from destruction, and plagues of vermin have been kept in check.

Many cats have been employed officially by the British government, some of them with the civil service where they are paid a salary. Barracks, offices, museums, factories, and shipyards all have cats as lifelong residents.

Austria employs cats in an official capacity. Hong Kong once made it compulsory for a cat to be quartered in every home. The national printing office of France boasts a large staff of felines. The cost of caring for cats is included in the budget of the United States postal department.

Big freezing plants in Pittsburgh, Pennsylvania, installed cats in the belief that the rodent problem would be solved; but the rats matched the effort by adapting themselves to the cold. They could not be caught, trapped, or poisoned. Finally, the problem was met by importing sturdy cats from Alaska, who could withstand not only the cold but also the harsh existence in continual darkness.

Cats and People

A deep affection between people and cats has produced numerous instances of loyalty and love.

Cats show a marked sympathy toward prisoners. The third Earl of Southampton, when sentenced to solitary confinement by Queen Elizabeth for a marriage which she did not favor, was

befriended by a cat who found him in the Tower and stayed at his side until he was released.

During the fifteenth century a cat carried pigeons and other fare for her master whom Richard III had thrown into prison.

Among great statesmen who loved their cats are Wolsey, Mazarin, Richelieu, and Chateaubriand. Mohammed so loved his cat that he cut his robe rather than disturb the sleep of his favored Muessa.

Presidents have shown warm affinity toward their cats. Thomas Jefferson, Abraham Lincoln, and George Washington were attracted by the quality of independence inherent in the cat. A big black cat named Nelson was Winston Churchill's constant companion during his times at home. Pope Gregory the Great, who lived in the sixth century, tamed a number of cats to whom he was warmly attached.

Many authors of distinction had their favorite cats. Victor Hugo, Émile Zola, Pierre Loti, and Anatole France, as well as Dickens, Lafcadio Hearn, Louis Untermeyer, and Carl Van Vechten found their cats to be both a comfort and an inspiration.

Jenny Lind acknowledged that her earliest audience was her favorite cat. Sacchini, the composer, admitted that he worked best when his cats ranged themselves in full view of his desk. Paderewski, inwardly nervous at his first London debut, turned to his cat seated on a chair beside him and asked the animal to wish him luck. The cat replied by leaping into his lap and purring loudly, as if to give him courage. Paderewski repaid the gesture by playing Scarlatti's "Cat's Fugue" as an encore piece.

Superstitions

A cat loves warmth. No doubt this is where the superstition had its conception that a cat sucks the breath of an infant. The fact remains that the crib or bassinet is soft and warming and inviting. Its call to comfort is irresistible.

There are those who declare that a cat washing herself is a sign of good weather. Napoleon, cat resident in Baltimore, was recognized as a weather prophet, and his forecasts were published in the *Baltimore Sun*. His career began when he predicted rain after a long, forty-day drought, in rebuttal to the official weather report, which predicted continual dry days. It rained—and Napoleon became the first cat reporter on record.

The cat who washes her fur against the grain is supposedly predicting stormy weather. In Germany, a superstition persists that if a citizen mistreats his cat, he will go to his grave in a storm.

Various locales have their own superstitions.

Maine claims that rain will pour if a cat is seen scratching a fence.

New York claims clear weather when a cat washes her face in the morning.

New England insists that a cat washing her face in the morning indicates a storm before night.

Killing a cat in New England is sure to produce bad luck. And a farmer who kills his cat will bring death to his cows and chickens.

If a cat comes in three or more colors, it will bring good luck to residents of both Kansas and Washington.

A dark-nosed cat brings prosperity to each who owns one in New England. A white cat brings poverty. In Alabama, should a cat wash his face in the presence of several people, the first person upon whom he casts his eye will be married within weeks.

Superstitions abound, but facts remain as facts—the main one being that the cat has carved a monumental record of achievements.

Retirement Homes for Animals

Pets sometimes find themselves homeless after years with a loving family because the family can no longer keep the animal for reasons that are beyond the control of the family. Older pet owners can die or become too ill to care for a loved cat or dog, or have to move to a nursing home where pets are not allowed. And from time to time a stray enters our lives that we can no longer keep—but we don't want to send it to the pound to be euthanized. When pets need the love and care their owners can no longer give them, there's now a humane alternative to putting the animal to sleep: a retirement home.

Several marvelous homes are available in different parts of the country. Among the best:

Animal Haven Farm, c/o Associated Humane Societies, 124 Evergreen Avenue, Newark, New Jersey 07114; (201) 824-7080. Pets live in well-cared-for facilities and have room to enjoy themselves with other animals if they're able. The cost for lifetime care in this loving atmosphere is based on the age of your pet. Good homes are sought for animals (a careful screening process is used), but if an animal is unable to be placed he can live out his life in comfort at the Farm. A tag can be ordered for each of your pets which reads: "In the event of the death of my owner, please immediately call Associated Humane Societies." The telephone number is listed. A wallet card is also provided in case you become incapacitated while away from home. As soon as they receive a call, AHS arranges for your pet to be picked up and transported to Animal Haven Farm.

Peace Plantation, P.O. Box 837, Leesburg, Virginia 22075, is a facility of the National Humane Education Society. Animals get complete care and plenty of love for the rest of their natural lives. A new plantation facility is being planned that will shelter more animals and offer services to pet owners. Send for their quarterly journal.

Cat Retirement Center, c/o National Cat Protection Society, P.O. Box 6065, Long Beach, California 90806; (213) 436-3162, operates a huge cat shelter where more than a hundred cats can live together without being crowded. For a $250 placement fee, the Center will feed and house your cat and try to find a good home for it. If you prefer not to have it adopted, other arrangements can be made. A veterinarian checks all cats every week, and pets must be tested before arrival for Feline Leukemia and Feline Infectious Peritonitis to avoid spreading the diseases to the other cats. Loving, complete care is the hallmark of the center. Send for more information.

Kent Animal Shelter, Inc., River Road, Calverton, New York 11933; (516) 727-5731, provides lifetime care in a ranch setting on nearly two acres along the Peconic River. Pets receive loving care in a homelike atmosphere from "foster parents" who live at the ranch. No pet is caged; all receive complete veterinary surveillance and are allowed to live out their natural lives unless there is extreme and unbearable pain. The shelter is self-supporting and exists through the bequests of pets' owners.

Friends of Cats, Inc., P.O. Box 1613, Lakeside, California 92040, also offers lifelong care. Lifetime cats mix with the general cat shelter population. Write for a fact sheet.

Check with your local humane society or SPCA for the names of other retirement centers in your area. New ones are springing up regularly. Carefully check out all facilities before you decide where your pet will be happiest. If you're dealing with a center in another part of the country, ask for photos and plenty of information about the organization running the facility.

The word tabby was derived from a kind of taffeta, or ribbed silk, which when calendered or what is now termed "watered," is by that process covered with wavy lines. This stuff, in bygone times, was often called "tabby," hence the cat with lines or markings on its fur was called a "tabby" cat.

—Harrison Weir,
in *Our Cats and All About Them*

Some people say that cats are sneaky, evil and cruel. True, and they have many other fine qualities as well.

—Missy Dizick and Mary Bly,
in *Dogs Are Better Than Cats*

One of the fattest cats on record was Spice, who lived in Ridgefield, Connecticut. He tipped the scales at forty-three pounds in 1974, his fattest year. He died in 1977.

Dogs rush in where cats fear to tread.
—Anonymous

It is difficult to obtain the friendship of a cat. It is a philosophic animal, strange, holding to its habits, friend of order and cleanliness and one that does not place its affections thoughtlessly. It wishes only to be your friend (if you are worthy) and not your slave. It retains its free will and will do nothing that it considers unreasonable.

Seraphita remained for long hours immobile on a cushion, not sleeping, following with her eyes with an extreme intensity of attention scenes invisible to simple mortals. Her elegance, her distinction, aroused the idea of aristocracy; within her race she was at least a duchess. She doted on perfumes; with little spasms of pleasure she bit handkerchiefs impregnated with scent, she wandered among flasks on the dressing-table, and if she had been allowed to, would willingly have worn powder.

—Theophile Gautier, *La Menagerie Intime*

And God spake unto Noah, and to his sons with him, saying, and I, behold, I establish my covenant with you, and with your seed after you; and with every living creature that is with you, of the fowl, of the cattle, and of every beast of the earth with you; from all that go out of the ark, to every beast of the earth.

—Genesis 9:8–10

Confession

I've been named Poosie, and
I am spoiled
Thoroughly, thoroughly spoiled, and I like it.
And don't let anyone tell you different.
I lie upon the softest cushions,
Under the downiest covers
And love every moment.
I get the cream off the top of the milk every day
And special double thick, heavy on Sundays,
And I lap it up.
My owner is besotted.
She hugs and kisses me
And carries me around with her all day,
And talks to me
And I enjoy it.
I'm spoiled rotten, and, friends,
That's the life.
Whatever I want, I cry for,
Crab, lobster, caviar, fish roes, sardines, filet, white meat
     of chicken,
You name it,
She's got it,
I get it.
I don't want to work, or hunt.
If ten snow-white mice were to saunter past my nose,
I wouldn't lift a paw.
I'm greedy, graceless, shameless, lazy,
And luxury loving.
Everything that comes my way I take,
And yell for more.
I'm spoiled useless.
I admit it.
And I adore it.

—Paul Gallico

Leo the Lionhearted

by Susan DeVore Williams

"Leo the Lionhearted": That was the name I gave him because of his king-sized roar and feisty attitude. He may have *looked* like an ordinary Siamese cat, but the heart of a jungle monarch beat within his fawn-colored breast. And if ever an animal lived up to his name, Leo did.

His eyes first met mine through the window of a pet shop in Minneapolis on a cold spring day in 1964. All the kittens in the window tumbled playfully and seemed active and healthy, but when I put a hand into the midst of them, Leo was the one that turned from his play, rubbed himself ecstatically against my fingers, and gazed up at me with eager eyes. The tiny pupils

opened like the lenses of cameras to drink me in. "Pick me, me, me!" he seemed to yowl with his outsized Siamese voice. I glanced at the hand-lettered card on the wall that described the kittens: "Seal-point Siamese, born February 14, 1964, first shots complete." How symbolic, I thought. A living Valentine.

Leo was a surprise to me from his first day under our roof. I'd never had a cat before—we'd had cocker spaniels when I was small, and later my brother had a mutt named Bearcat. As an adult I'd had a bird, but a cat—well, a cat was the pet my husband and I had decided on because cats were independent. Cats didn't need the kind of attention dogs required. They used litter boxes instead of the yard, didn't have to be walked all the time, ate very little, and in general seemed like a realistic pet for two childless people who were away from home five workdays a week. I also reasoned that I wouldn't get too attached to a cat—they're so aloof, after all—and I'd be spared the sadness I'd experienced when the dogs in my childhood had died. A cat would not invite such an emotional commitment, I thought. It wouldn't want to get too close, and that suited me just fine.

But Leo had different ideas. His first night in our apartment I showed him his comfy new wicker cat bed in the living room, where he had easy access to everything he needed. Or so I thought. From ten o'clock until midnight he stood on the other side of the closed door to our bedroom and howled like a 300-pound bobcat, conveying to his idiot owners the message that closed doors would not be tolerated. I opened the door to chastise him and watched the furry little tyrant streak into the room and leap weightlessly onto our bed. There he immediately curled up, blinked at us innocently, and went to sleep. My husband, disgruntled to find himself sharing our double bed with a cat that had its own luxuriously cushioned bed, managed to nudge him off several times. Leo only threw him an annoyed glare and stalked back to his chosen spot between us. Having claimed his rights, he would not give them up. And he had infinite patience in training us.

Leo was to be an indoor cat. I'd learned from books that altered cats are perfectly happy staying indoors their whole lives, and can live nearly twice as long as they otherwise would. "People think

Day, 1985, he had survived still another infection and a move to a new home—and a new family. He was firmly in command of a household that now included my new husband, Richard, and his three animals. Spotty, an eighteen-pound cat of undetermined origin, gave Leo a wide berth and plenty of respect. Chewy, the eighty-pound golden lab/shepherd mix, yearned to make friends, but Leo was accustomed to his privacy and spurned all his advances. Dusty, the little fifteen-year-old mutt of Dick's household, was too blind and deaf to know that another creature had invaded her turf. Leo, reigning over this expanded kingdom with great equanimity, continued to thrive.

And I had decided—with a lot of encouragement from my husband, a deeply committed Christian—that I should finally obey the "calling" I'd felt all my life to make writing my career. Christian writing, specifically. By 1985 I had become a full-time professional with many articles in print, and Leo's story had been told to millions of people through *Guideposts* magazine.

On Leo's birthday, Valentine's Day, I got up early and read his own story to him. (He loved to hear about his own accomplishments. Even a missionary cat has his character flaws.) I'd known that he was growing more feeble, but he seemed strong and eager for petting that day. I stroked him as I continued to read, moving on to the Bible and drawing the usual blissful purrs when I got into the Psalms. *Amazing*, I thought. He still purred when I read, though his vet claimed he was now stone deaf and would soon be blind.

"Leo," I told him, "it's getting close. I can feel it. I know that one of these mornings I'll come in and find that you've gone to sleep and can't wake up." I began to cry. "I know it has to happen, because you can't live forever. But I'll miss you so much! What will I do without you, Leo?"

I looked around the room. My home, now. Leo's home. I tried to remember what it was like before Leo had been part of every home I'd known. Twenty-one years. My oldest, most loyal friend, Leo. Even with a marvelous, sensitive husband and the comfort his animals would bring, a big, empty space would be left when Leo was gone.

Gone—gone where, I wondered. Most of the Christians I knew

dismissed the notion that animals could have immortal souls. I did not dismiss it, but that morning, on Leo's twenty-first birthday, I needed more than that.

"Lord," I whispered, "I need to *know*. I need to be sure that Leo will be with You when he leaves me. I think I'm finally able to trust You on blind faith about everything else, but I have to know that much. *Please*." Leo's purrs mingled with the sounds of birds awakening in the early light. He looked at me with his "More, please" look, so I picked up the Bible again. "Let's go," I told him. "We'll start at the beginning."

When I reached the thirtieth verse of the first chapter of Genesis, I knew God was trying to communicate with me: ". . . to every beast of the earth, and to every fowl of the air, and to every thing that creepeth upon the earth, wherein there is a living soul, I have given every green herb for meat: and it was so. . . . and God saw every thing that he had made, and behold, it was very good" (*See* Genesis 1:30, 31).

Wherein there is a living soul? I smiled, hugging Leo. He squinted at me with pleasure, his purr rumbling through the room. "Okay, Lord," I said, grabbing a legal pad and pencil next to my easy chair. "I'm ready to listen."

For the next two hours Leo and I picked our way through the Bible. I don't know quite how I found all the verses I copied that morning, but by the time we'd finished, the whole page was covered with passages that confirmed for me that the animals do, indeed, belong to God, and that He loves them deeply. I grinned at Leo. "Now, old man," I said, "all that remains is for us to find out if you're really going to be waiting to greet me in heaven. And for that I can wait." Leo blinked and hopped off my lap, tail up. It was going to be all right, I thought.

I went to the kitchen and opened a can of Nine Lives Liver and Creamed Gravy, expecting Leo to come at the sound of the can opener. He didn't. I walked to where he was sitting, sphinx-like, on his heating pad, and put his bowl in front of him. "It's your birthday, so you're entitled to breakfast in bed," I said. He blinked at me and purred but made no move to eat. It surprised me. Except when he was very ill, Leo always had an appetite for liver and creamed gravy. But he was fine, so what was wrong?

By evening Leo still had eaten nothing. His water bowl showed he'd had nothing to drink. I stared at him, puzzled. "What's wrong, old friend? Is your twenty-first birthday too much for you? Are you on strike because we didn't throw a party?"

The following day Leo still refused to eat or drink, budging from his heating pad only occasionally to stagger unsteadily to his litter box. I picked him up and stood him on the table in front of the sofa, where his favorite water cup was kept, but he only stared at the water and gave me a worn-out look. There was also a "Tree of Life" on that table. I had modeled it to resemble an Israeli artist's depiction of the Tree of Life from the Garden of Eden. Ever the religious fanatic, Leo seemed to love that tree. Or perhaps it was the fact that it gleamed and shimmered with hundreds of tiny gold-metallic leaves that hung from golden wire branches. I'd grown used to seeing Leo take a drink from the cup and then bat the leaves with his paw as he finished. It was Leo's tree. At night I'd walk into the darkened family room and see Leo's eyes glowing in the dark, and I'd know he was standing on that table getting a drink and playing with the Tree of Life. But today he didn't seem to notice it at all. I rustled the leaves to catch his attention, but he ignored it.

I called Leo's new vet, a remarkable, compassionate man who'd marveled that a cat could live so long and survive so much. "He's the oldest cat I've ever seen," he'd told us. I explained the situation and told him that I was especially worried because I had set up a two-day trip to do an important interview, and the trip would be difficult to cancel. Richard had urgent business, as well. There would be nobody to take care of Leo except for the three or four times my husband said he'd run home from his office to check him. The vet asked me to bring Leo to his clinic for a thorough exam. When he was done he, too, seemed puzzled.

"His kidneys are still functioning. I was afraid from what you said that they had stopped. He's weak and listless and very dehydrated, but I can't understand what's going on. His heart is fairly strong. It's almost as if he's just shutting down his body systems and has decided to die. No eating, no drinking, no elimination—that really isn't good. And I don't know quite what to do other than to keep him here and put in an IV. If he gets fluids, we can keep him going for a few days and perhaps, in that time, he'll get hungry and want to eat again." He smiled. "With this cat, I'd say nothing is impossible."

"I can cancel my trip and stay with him," I said. "I can give him fluids myself, with an eye dropper. He might be more comfortable at home." The vet had read Leo's story and knew I'd do anything necessary to keep him alive, but he disagreed.

"No, he's not aware of much of anything right now. He'll be comfortable here. I'll be here almost all the time, and I'll check him in the night several times. And you couldn't get enough fluid into him with a dropper at home. It has to go into his veins. He really needs to be here—that is, if you want to try to save him." He looked at me and knew the answer.

I hugged Leo good-bye. He didn't seem to recognize me, but I left him feeling relieved that he was in loving hands. If he was to survive again, he had to be at the vet's for at least two days. I decided to go ahead with my trip. I could keep in touch and drive home, if necessary, in less than four hours.

The interview went well, and I was glad I hadn't stayed home. My phone calls home told me that Leo was holding his own. The Lord definitely wanted me to do that story, I mused, so I was confident that Leo would be alive when I returned. On the drive home I talked to the Lord about Leo. I reminded Him that I'd asked Him dozens of times to allow Leo to die at home, sleeping, curled up on his heating pad or on my lap. I was more certain than ever that if it was time for Leo to go, God would work it out that way.

Shortly after I walked in the door at home the phone rang. My husband came in the house as I picked up the receiver and heard the veterinarian's voice. "Thank God you're home," he said. "I'm sorry, but just in the last hour or so Leo has taken a dramatic turn for the worse. He was doing pretty well, but for some reason he's suddenly started going downhill in a hurry. I think you should come over right away."

My husband saw from the look on my face what was happening. He put his arms around me and held me as I cried. Soon I realized that he was crying, too. "Let's pray for Leo," he said.

The strangest thought flickered through my mind in that moment. I thought, *If this had happened five or ten years ago, I would have had no one to cry with.* I remembered that my first husband had never understood or shared the deep feelings I had for Leo. When Leo was sick, I'd always taken care of him alone. When I'd thought Leo was dying, I'd been terrified by the thought that I'd have to bury him alone. My first husband had liked and enjoyed Leo, but I'd known I would be the only one to mourn him. Now, confronted with the reality of Leo's imminent death, I was with a man who loved him almost as much as I did. And he was going to be there to help me through it.

As he drove the few blocks to the vet's I told Richard that I thought we should bring Leo home, that I knew God was not going to make me take the responsibility for his death. Leo was going to simply go to sleep that night as he always did, and not wake up tomorrow. That was how I'd prayed for it, and that was how it was going to be. My husband said, "God gave him to you, and it's your decision. So we'll bring him home if that's what you want, no matter what the vet says."

As soon as I saw Leo, I knew it was nearly over. He showed no sign that he knew me, and the vet explained that his brain wasn't functioning normally, so he couldn't be aware of much that was happening. The IV was still in his arm, but his body was nothing but fur and bone. His eyes were glazed. I rubbed his chin as he loved to have it rubbed, but there was no response. The vet quietly came to my side and put his hand on Leo's head.

"His systems are shutting down rapidly," he said. "In a very short time he's going to be in a lot of pain. Right now there isn't any. But it's not going to be pleasant for him if you let it go on any longer."

The words didn't seem real. "No," I said. "I'm taking him home tonight. I'll sit up with him until morning." The vet looked at my husband, who was by this time bent over Leo's frail body, gently stroking him. Richard had worked in an animal hospital during college; this scene was not new to him. He came around the table to me and said to the doctor, "Give us a few minutes alone, will you?" The vet and his assistant left the room.

Richard didn't speak for a while; he just held me while I cried. I said, "I wanted to have one more night with him. One more chance to let him sleep on my lap. Is that so much to ask? God can't make me kill him! That's the one thing I've asked over and over again. He can't ask that of me!" My husband finally said, "He belongs to you. We'll take him home if that's what you really want."

I looked at Leo. I touched him gently, afraid that even my touch would hurt him. "No," I said finally. "I can't let him go through the pain that's ahead. The one last thing I can do for him is to help him die without that."

We prayed, and I couldn't stop shaking. Finally I stroked Leo's head and said, "Lord, I give him back to You. It's Your turn to take care of Leo. Thank You for letting me have him all these years." I told Leo I loved him. It was only minutes later that the anesthetic was administered as we held Leo and I rubbed his chin and cheeks. In perhaps six or seven seconds, his heart stopped beating. Leo the Lionhearted was gone.

We went home, where my husband made a special box cushioned with Leo's favorite towels and pads, and we buried him next to the new rose bush I'd planted in the fall. My husband read aloud the sheet of Bible verses I'd copied on Leo's birthday just five days before, ending with my favorite one of them all: ". . . ask now the beasts, and they shall teach thee; and the fowls of the air, and they shall tell thee: or speak to the earth, and it shall teach thee: and the fishes of the sea shall declare unto thee. Who knoweth not in all these that the hand of the Lord hath wrought this? In whose hand is the soul of every living thing, and the breath of all mankind" (Job 12:7–10).

The next few days and nights were very hard. It was excruciatingly difficult to walk into the family room, which Leo had made his own, expecting to see his eyes gleaming out of the darkness—only to see nothing. Leo's water glass was gone, but the Tree of Life remained. It was a painful reminder. My husband asked if we shouldn't put the Tree somewhere else. "No," I said, "I somehow have to stop crying every time I see it. I have to be able to live where Leo lived without being sad about everything connected to him."

Richard was sensitive and loving, letting me do crazy things without making me feel crazy. He let me stand at the small mound by the rose bush and talk to Leo, let me cry when a cat food commercial came on TV, let me sit in the dark at night and whisper to God, "I can't stand it, I just can't. Why didn't You do what I asked? Why did I have to be the one to make him die? I need to hold him one more time, Lord. I need to see his eyes one more time. I have to know he's okay. Help me believe that." But there were no reassurances coming from God. I felt that God was too far away for me to reach.

On the third night after Leo died, I tossed sleeplessly until about 3:00 A.M. I hadn't slept much the two nights before and had awakened with nightmares about Leo. I was afraid to sleep, I think, because I dreaded the nightmares more than anything else. I sat in the bedroom chair for a while, thinking. I had work to do, stories to write, and I couldn't seem to get past the fact of Leo's death. Why couldn't I imagine him in heaven with the Lord, happily playing? Perhaps he was batting at the leaves of the *real* Tree of Life by now. But it didn't help. *I need him tonight, Lord,* I thought. *I need something to tell me he's really with You. Is that wrong? I should be able to trust You by now. Leo would be upset with me, wouldn't he?*

I wanted to read to distract myself but didn't want to awaken my husband. If I went into the family room, I'd have that awful, sinking feeling when I expected to see Leo's eyes gazing at me and found they weren't there. But I made myself walk down the hall anyway, and turned into the family room muttering to myself that I had to stop being such a basket case. I forced myself to look directly at the table where Leo's eyes usually gleamed, steeling myself for the moment of grief.

What I saw absolutely stunned me. There they were. There were his eyes—glowing from the table as they always did, shiny and glittery as gold coins against the blackness of the darkened room. I was speechless. I stared, transfixed. Was I having a hallucination?

"Leo," I whispered, "is that you?" Our other cat was in her own lair in the other room, I knew, and the dogs were asleep. These eyes could belong to no one but Leo. Finally I tiptoed toward them. They seemed to be gazing at me happily, as Leo gazed when he was feeling his best. Then they blinked. I groped for the light and flipped the switch as I continued to stare at Leo's shining eyes.

It was the Tree of Life. Two of the golden leaves had caught a bit of light from somewhere in the darkened house, and it was those leaves that had been shining out of the dark at me. I sat down, laughing quietly, shaken to the core. Of course it couldn't have been Leo. I knew that. But how did those leaves glow like that when I could find no light source? And how could they look so much like his eyes? I'd have sworn. . . .

I sat down on the spot where Leo liked to spend his days, on the big, comfy sofa. I looked at the Tree again and felt a peculiar, welcome warmth spread through my mind and body. Suddenly, I knew.

Leo the Lionhearted, my missionary cat, was alive. He hadn't left me forever—he had just gone home on furlough to collect his commendations for extraordinary valor on the field. He'd done what he'd been sent to do all those twenty-one years ago. I'd learned all that Leo had come to teach me. He'd been faithful to his calling, and his example had made me want to be faithful to mine. He had "come of age" and it was time for him to leave, but God had used even his departure to bring home one final, exquisite lesson in trust. He did not—and would not—wrench Leo from me without my consent; He waited for the exact moment when I finally had enough strength to give him back of my own free will.

God knew that if He'd taken Leo from me in the way I'd always prayed He would, I'd never have accepted it. Instead, when the time came, He and Leo had brought me to the point where I was ready to say, "Here, Lord, I give him back to You."

And I had done it. I had done what I was absolutely certain I could never do. Out of love for Leo, to be sure, and out of compassion. But also because of the trust Leo had helped me build during our twenty-one years together. That trust in God's ultimate purpose had enabled me to reach beyond my own pain and anguish to give Leo back to God.

I smiled and headed for the bedroom, sure that I'd sleep at last. Leo was alive in my heart again, and I knew he'd be there forever.

Think of her beautiful gliding form,
Her tread that would scarcely crush a worm,
And her soothing song by the winter fire,
Soft as the dying throb of a lyre.

—William Wordsworth

A Childlike Faith

by Patricia Salisbury

The bright sun of that August morning warmed the rough wooden steps of the back porch where I sat with my two daughters, shelling a bucket of peas. It was hard to believe we were so soon on the downhill side of summer, that Grandmother Treasure would by now have been on her way back to her own home—except that she wouldn't be going back on schedule. She probably wouldn't be going back at all.

As if picking my thoughts out of the air, 7-year-old Julie suddenly asked: "When will Great Grandma come out of the hospital?"

Two pairs of wide blue eyes, innocent and questioning, waited for my answer.

"Great Grandma is a very old lady," I said slowly. "And she's very sick."

"I know that," Julie said, almost impatiently. "But she's going to get all better. I asked God to fix her."

Uh-oh.

"That's good, Julie," I said. "I'm glad you talked to God about Great Grandma." Stalling, I reached for another handful of pods. My grandmother was seriously ill. The entire family was dutifully praying for her recovery, while preparing for her death.

"Sometimes, though," I went on, "it isn't that simple. Sometimes, no matter how much we pray, sick people don't get better. Sometimes sick people die."

Julie considered this. "No," she declared, very certain. "Great Grandma's going to get all better. I just wondered how soon God will let her out of the hospital."

Two weeks later, surprising Great Grandma, her doctor and all of her family—amazing everyone, I think, except Julie—Great Grandma was released from the hospital.

After that, whenever things seemed too hopeless even for

prayer, I called to mind my grandmother's recovery and the faith of a child, and I prayed anyway.

When Julie turned 12 several years later, she plunged into the turbulence of adolescence. On the first Friday of school that year she stormed into the house 20 minutes late. "I hate that bus driver!" she shrilled, slamming her lunch box against the counter.

I put down the potato I was peeling. "Let's have no more of that kind of talk," I scolded. "Hatred—"

"I know," she interrupted in a mocking voice. "Don't hate the person, hate the person's sin. Well, I hate her anyway!" So intense was Julie's anger that she could not muster a smile even for Tiger, stroking himself against her legs and gazing up at her with adoration.

Tiger was Julie's cat from the time Julie was 9. They spent every possible moment together—she with bubbling laughter, sparkling blue eyes and bouncing brown curls; he with strutting walk and tail held high, his heart in his eyes.

"Julie," I began again, half pleading and half angry myself. But she scooped Tiger from the floor and stalked quickly from the kitchen.

I sighed, feeling helpless. Scenes such as this were becoming more frequent as Julie began to leave childhood behind. The influence of church, Sunday school and prayers seemed, thus far, not enough.

That night Tiger disappeared. My husband, Brian, let him out at 10 P.M., as usual. But the next morning Tiger was nowhere to be seen.

It was not the first time Tiger had pulled this stunt. Each time, I urged Julie to pray for his safe return. I thought it would be a good way for a child to learn to talk with God. Each time, Tiger came home within three days, hungry and repentant. I remember one time after Tiger returned when Julie, cuddling Tiger on her lap, suddenly asked, "Mom, do you think God sent Tiger home, or did Tiger just come home on his own?" I answered carefully, "God always hears our prayers." God heard—I still believed that sincerely. But might He not have more important things to do than chase after one silly cat?

This time Tiger did not come back in three days. When a week had gone by, Julie came to me as I was clearing away the wreck of Saturday brunch. She was still in her nightgown, her hair a mass of tangles, and I was immediately annoyed. She knew we would be leaving for town in a few minutes.

"Tiger's never been gone this long before," she said abruptly. "I'm worried about him."

"I'm sure he'll be all right," I told her. "Hand me that glass, will you?"

"But he's been gone all week," she insisted. "Don't you *care?*"

"Of course I care." My reply was edged with impatience. I did care—that Tiger was missing, that Julie was so concerned. But at that moment, I also cared about cleaning up my messy kitchen before going shopping.

"Then isn't there something we can do?" Julie demanded.

"Certainly," I said, still impatient. "You can pray."

Julie shrugged with impatience of her own. "Sure," she said. "But isn't there anything we can really *do?*"

Had I not been so rushed, I might have caught the implication of that question. But maybe not.

"We could try an ad in the lost and found section of the paper," I suggested.

"Nobody around here would bother to answer it, even if they did see Tiger," Julie scoffed.

"Yes they will," I said. "We'll offer a $25 reward." My mouth was leading a life all its own. I knew we couldn't afford that kind of extravagance.

"Really?"

"Yes," I assured her. "And I'll phone the neighbors and ask them to let us know if they see Tiger."

I was not looking forward to the good-natured scorn I would encounter in those telephone calls. To our farming neighbors, a cat was a cat was a cat, and no one cat was worth any amount of bother. But they were all good neighbors, and I knew they would help if they could.

"Now you run along and get dressed," I said.

"Okay," Julie agreed, and headed out the doorway.

"And Julie," I called. "Remember what I said about praying, too." Sure, she was becoming a teenager, but she could still talk to God about her lost cat.

"Okay Mom," she responded.

Thanksgiving week came, cold, wet and blustery—and still no Tiger. Two evenings before Thanksgiving, we kindled a fire in the living room heater, and it was warm and cozy there when I came in from clearing away the supper dishes.

Julie was sitting quietly in my rocking chair with the photograph album open in her lap. Coming closer, I could see the snapshots of Julie and Tiger taken that summer. But Julie was staring blankly into the rain-swept darkness beyond the window.

"A penny for your thoughts," I said gently. I thought she might be crying, but when she turned to look at me, her eyes were dry. "I was just thinking about Tiger," she said, and looked down at the photos. "He was such a good cat. We had so much fun together."

My throat ached with grief for Julie, and I felt that helpless desperation every mother knows when her child is in pain. "He could still come home, you know."

Julie shook her head slowly—she wasn't being stubborn or argumentative, just resigned. "No, Mom. He's been gone for five weeks. And it's so cold. Where would he sleep, or stay warm and dry? What would he eat all this time? He must be dead. But I just wish I knew for sure what happened to him." She stopped for a minute and turned her face to the window, then went on.

"If I knew he died quickly—run over by a car, or something—it wouldn't be so bad. But I keep thinking of him caught in a trap, maybe, and dying slowly—cold, and hungry, and afraid, and thinking that I would come and save him. He trusted me. I don't want him to have died thinking that I let him down."

"Whatever happened with Tiger, it's in the Lord's hands," I told her.

"Sure," she replied weakly.

The conversation stayed with me and stirred reverberating echoes of the past: *"Sometimes, no matter how much we pray. . . ."* Then, Julie had prayed with the simple faith of a child, and her prayers had been answered. Now her faith seemed to be weakening. It was my turn to pray for Tiger as she had prayed for Great Grandma.

Late that night I turned desperately to the Lord: "Dear Father, please send Tiger home. I know You care about little sparrows, so I'm sure You care about cats. But I'm not asking for Tiger's sake alone. I'm asking for Julie, too. Please don't let her be hurt this way, when she is finding life so confusing. We often do not understand the things You do and must rely on Your promise that all things work together for good for them that love You. I'm Julie's mother, and I can see that she is being hurt, and I can't see any good in it. Please send Tiger home. In Jesus' name, amen."

The next day we conducted the last search. We drove the rough gravel roads, peering through the rain to check the ditches. Julie and her sister trudged through muddy fields to search abandoned farm buildings—calling, listening, calling again. Finally, wet and cold and discouraged, we gave up. Tiger must be dead. It was stupid to go on hoping.

Brian woke up early Thanksgiving morning and hurried downstairs to light a fire in the kitchen cookstove. I snuggled deeper under the sheep's wool quilt for a few more minutes of warmth and laziness. But a moment later I heard Brian come quickly back up the stairs and into the girls' bedroom.

"Julie," I heard him gently say, "Do you recognize this fellow?"

"Tiger!" she cried.

Even from my room I could hear Tiger's answering "merrow."

"Thank You, God," I whispered.

"Oh, Mom!" Julie called. "Tiger's back! It's Thanksgiving morning, and God really did bring him home!"

As her voice rang out with the joy of certainty, my eyes glistened with tears of another joy—the assurance that God sent my daughter's beloved pet back so that she—and I—would know again that His ear still hears, and His hand still answers, the faith of a child and a childlike faith.

Did You Know . . .

The cat's tongue can reach every part of its body except the center of the back of the neck and between the shoulder blades.

Cats' nose pads are like human fingerprints. No two are alike.

A cat's saliva contains something called the epidermal growth factor. This aids in healing when the cat licks its wounds.

The giraffe, the camel, and the cat all move the same way: the front and back legs on one side first, then the front and back legs on the other side. It would seem that only the cat has perfected the style.

Maybe in Bethlehem

The ass was there in Bethlehem,
And flocks of wooly sheep,
But I like to think a little cat
Purred the Babe to sleep.

An ox was there, and other beasts
Too large to come too near.
But a little cat could curl up close
And cause the Child no fear.

And maybe Jesus clutched its fur,
And maybe Mary smiled
To see the small one lying there
Beside the Holy Child.

—Margaret Hillert

A re not two sparrows sold for a farthing? And one of them shall not fall to the ground without your father.
—Matthew 10:29

The wolf also shall dwell with the lamb, and the leopard shall lie down with the kid; and the calf and the young lion and the fatling together; and a little child shall lead them. And the cow and the bear shall feed; their young ones shall lie down together: and the lion shall eat straw like the ox. . . . They shall not hurt nor destroy in all my holy mountain: for the earth shall be full of the knowledge of the Lord, as the waters cover the sea.

—From the biblical prophecy describing the Kingdom of God which will one day come to earth through the Messiah (Isaiah 11:6, 7, 9).

A Prayer for Animals

Hear our humble prayer, O God, for our friends the animals, especially for animals whgo are suffering; for any that are hunted or lost or deserted or frightened or hungry; for all that must be put to death. We entreat for them all Thy Mercy and pity, and for those who deal with them we ask a heart of compassion and gentle hands and kindly words. Make us ourselves to be true friends to animals and so to share the blessings of the merciful. Amen.

—Dr. Albert Schweitzer

Acknowledgments

The author and Fleming H. Revell Company thank the following authors, publishers, and agents whose cooperation and permission to reprint have made possible the preparation of this book. All possible care has been taken to trace the ownership of every selection included and to make full acknowledgment for its use. If any errors have accidentally occurred, they will be corrected in subsequent editions, provided notification is sent to the publishers.

"The Cat in the Conspiracy "by Aletha Lindstrom is reprinted with permission from *Guideposts* magazine, copyright © 1983 by Guideposts Associates, Inc., Carmel, N.Y. 10512.

"Catalog" by Rosalie Moore, reprinted by permission; copyright © 1940, 1968, the *New Yorker* magazine, Inc.

"Seeing-Eye Cats" by Brian McConnachie, from *Cat Catalog*, copyright © 1976 by Workman Publishing Company, New York. Reprinted with permission.

"Cat Bathing as a Martial Art" by Bud Herron, reprinted with permission from The *Saturday Evening Post* Society, a division of BFL&MS, Inc., copyright © 1985.

"Portrait—8 Weeks," copyright © 1963 by Margaret Hillert, reprinted by permission of the author.

"A Candle for Samantha," copyright © 1987 by Catherine Vanicek, appeared in *Cat Fancy* magazine and is reprinted by permission of the author.

"Night Cat," copyright © 1987 by Susan DeVore Williams.

"The Cat's Attention Span" by Stephen Baker, from *How to Live With a Neurotic Cat*, copyright © 1985. Reprinted by permission of Warner Books, New York.

"The Box" by Mary Louise Kitsen, reprinted with permission from *Guideposts* magazine, copyright © 1976 by Guideposts Associates, Inc., Carmel, N.Y. 10512.

"Here Among the Daffodils," copyright © 1966 Margaret Hillert, first published in *Cat Fancy* magazine. Reprinted by permission of the author.

"Learn the Cat Language," copyright © 1986 by Michael W. Fox, first appeared in *Boy's Life* magazine. Reprinted by permission of the author.

"Body Language" from *The Ultimate Cat Catalog,* copyright © 1986 by Lesley Sussman and Sally Bordwell, published by McGraw-Hill. Used by permission of the publisher.

"C. S. Lewis' Personal Thoughts about Animals" from *Letters to an American Lady* by C. S. Lewis. Copyright © 1967, William B. Eerdmans Publishing Co. Used by permission.

Information for "A Cat by Any Other Name" was supplied by Anderson Animal Shelter in Elgin, Illinois. Used by permission.

"Sweet Sam, Farewell," copyright © 1985 by Patty Johnson Cormaney, first appeared in *Trailer Life* magazine. Used by permission of the author.

"For a Very Old Cat," copyright © 1963 by Margaret Hillert, first appeared in *Lyric,* Fall 1963. Used with the author's permission.

"Stray," copyright © 1966 by Margaret Hillert, from *Pet Prose and Poems* (1966). Used with the author's permission.

"Kitty Love," copyright © 1985 by Patty Johnson Cormaney, first appeared in *Trailer Life* magazine. Reprinted with the author's permission.

"Application" by Paul Gallico reprinted from *Honorable Cat* by Paul Gallico. Copyright © 1972 by Paul Gallico and Mathemata Anstalt. Used by permission of Crown Publishers, Inc.

"Some People Say That Cats Are Sneaky ," from *Dogs Are Better Than Cats,* copyright © 1984 by Missy Dizick and Mary Bly. Used by permission of Doubleday & Company.

"10 Commandments of Pet Ownership," copyright © 1985 by Michael W. Fox, appeared in *Boy's Life* magazine. Reprinted with permission from the author.

"Test Your Pet I.Q." by Francis Sheridan Goulart reprinted with permission of The *Saturday Evening Post* Society, a division of BFL&MS, Inc., copyright © 1987.

"A Best Friend for Kevin" copyright © 1987 by Catherine Vanicek appeared in *Cats* magazine and is reprinted by permission of the author.

"The Cat's Page in History" by Beth Brown is adapted from *Cats* © 1970 by Beth Brown.

"Confession" by Paul Gallico from *Honorable Cat* by Paul Gallico. Copyright © 1972 by Paul Gallico and Mathemata Anstalt. Used by permission of Crown Publishers, Inc.

"Leo the Lionhearted," by Susan DeVore Williams, adapted from a story by the same name in *Guideposts* magazine, August 1984. Reprinted with permission from *Guideposts* magazine. Copyright © 1984 by Guideposts Associates, Inc., Carmel, N.Y. 10512.

"Maybe in Bethlehem," copyright © 1962 by Margaret Hillert, first appeared in the Denver *Post*. Used by permission of the author.

"A Childlike Faith" by Patricia Salisbury is used with permission from *Charisma & Christian Life* magazine, 190 N. Westmonte Drive, Altamonte Springs, FL 32714. Copyright 1988. Strang Communications Company.

Photos on pages 12, 28, 80, 116, and 159 are reprinted by permission of The Putnam Publishing Group from THE PETS ARE WONDERFUL FAMILY ALBUM by The Pets Are Wonderful Council. Copyright © 1984 by The Pets Are Wonderful Council.

Photo on page 19 is © FPG International/G. Randall.

Illustration on page 26 is a rubber stamp © 1988 by Marks of Distinction, Chicago, IL 60615. Used by permission.

Illustration on page 38 is a rubber stamp made by Patrick & Company, 560 Market Street, San Francisco, CA 94104. Used by permission.

Photos on pages 2, 50, 103 are © by Bill Engle Photography. Used by permission.

Illustration on page 113 is a rubber stamp © All Night Media, Inc., San Anselmo, CA 94960. Stamp drawing by Robert Bloomberg. Used by permission.

*W*hen a cat is alone she never purrs.

—Dr. Samuel Johnson

The author would enjoy hearing from readers with their own animal stories and photos. She regrets that the volume of mail may make it impossible for her to return photos or acknowledge correspondence. She may be addressed at P.O. Box 19822, Sacramento, CA 95819-0822.